D1585928

Sacred Edinburgh and Midlothian

SACRED PLACES SERIES

Sacred Edinburgh and Midlothian

SCOTLAND'S CHURCHES SCHEME

SAINT ANDREW PRESS
Edinburgh

First published in 2009 by
SAINT ANDREW PRESS
121 George Street
Edinburgh
EH2 4YN

ISBN 978 0 7152 0922 6

British Library Cataloguing in Publication Data
A catalogue record for this book is available from the British Library.

It is the publisher's policy to only use papers that are natural and recyclable and that
have been manufactured from timber grown in renewable, properly managed forests.
All of the manufacturing processes of the papers are expected to conform to the
environmental regulations of the country of origin.

Typeset in Enigma by Waverley Typesetters, Fakenham
Manufactured in Great Britain by Bell & Bain Ltd, Glasgow

BUCKINGHAM PALACE

As Patron of Scotland's Churches Scheme I warmly welcome this publication, particularly during this year of *Homecoming Scotland 2009*.

The story of the heritage and culture of Scotland would be lacking significantly without a strong focus on its churches and sacred sites. I am sure that this guidebook will be a source of information and enjoyment both to the people of Scotland and to our visitors during this memorable year.

Anne

Scotland's Churches Scheme

Scotland's Churches Scheme is an ecumenical charitable trust, providing an opportunity to access the nation's living heritage of faith by assisting the 'living' churches to:

- Promote spiritual understanding by enabling the public to appreciate all buildings designed for worship and active as living churches
- Work together with others to make the Church the focus of the community
- Open their doors with a welcoming presence
- Tell the story of the building (however old or new), its purpose and heritage (artistic, architectural and historical)
- Provide information for visitors, young and old

The Scheme has grown rapidly since its inception in 1994 and there are now more than 1200 churches in membership. These churches are spread across Scotland and across the denominations.

The *Sacred Scotland* theme promoted by Scotland's Churches Scheme focuses on the wish of both visitors and local communities to be able to access our wonderful range of church buildings in a meaningful way, whether the visit be occasioned by spiritual or heritage motivation or both. The Scheme can advise and assist member churches on visitor welcome, and with its range of 'how-to' brochures, provide information on research, presentation, security and other live issues. The Scheme, with its network of local representatives, encourages the opening of doors, the care of tourists and locals alike, and offers specific services such as the provision of grants for organ playing.

Sacred Scotland (www.sacredscotland.org.uk), the web-site of Scotland's Churches Scheme, opens the door to Scotland's story by exploring living traditions of faith in city, town, village and island across the country. The site is a portal to access information on Scotland's churches of all denominations and a starting point for your special journeys.

We are delighted to be working with Saint Andrew Press in the publication of this series of regional guides to Scotland's churches. This volume, *Edinburgh and Midlothian*, is one of three being published in 2009 (the others are *Fife and the Forth Valley* and *South-West Scotland*) to be followed by a further three books in 2010 and again in 2011 when the whole country will have been covered. We are grateful to the authors of the introductory articles: Professor John Hume, one of our Trustees, and Allan Maclean for their expert contributions to our understanding of sacred places.

The growth of 'spiritual tourism' worldwide is reflected in the million-plus people who visit Scotland's religious sites annually. We hope that the information in this book will be useful in bringing alive the heritage as well as the ministry of welcome which our churches offer. In the words of our President, Lady Marion Fraser: 'we all owe a deep debt of gratitude to the many people of vision who work hard and imaginatively to create a lasting and peaceful atmosphere which you will carry away with you as a special memory when you leave'.

Dr Brian Fraser
Director

Invitation to Pilgrimage

Edinburgh and Midlothian

"Edinburgh is a city of churches, as though it were a place of pilgrimage."
R. L. Stevenson

Edinburgh is the capital of Scotland and many of the great religious and spiritual events in the history of the nation have happened here. As a large and thriving city it is the home of many congregations who make up the rainbow of belief in today's world of pluriformity. To visit their buildings is both to learn of this rich variety and to be in touch, through faith, with the many generations who have passed this way before us.

In prehistoric times there is no doubt that people had their sacred places where they came to know of 'another world' beyond their own. Springs and wells were among their special places, including, perhaps, St Margaret's Well in Holyrood Park, and St Catherine's Well at Liberton.

Although there were probably some Christians among the Romans who controlled the lands between the Hadrian and Antonine Walls, when Christianity came to the Lothians it was part of the Kingdom of Northumbria. Of some significance was the mission of St Cuthbert and there is every reason to believe that St Cuthbert's Church (**22**) below the castle in Edinburgh is built on the site of the saint's original cell. Today the church contains many reminders of the saint, and the little chapel under the tower is a place of peace and contemplation in the heart of a great capital city.

St Margaret, Queen of Scotland, died at Edinburgh Castle, and the little chapel in her name (**2**) dates from about her time. It is now a focal point for anyone who honours St Margaret, and flowers are arranged there to the Glory of God and in her memory, by Scots of the name of Margaret. Generations of people have seen the chapel's Norman arch and to view it now is to bring one close to all those visitors of different ages who have come to seek Scotland's story at the castle.

St Margaret's saintly son, King David, founded many abbeys and religious houses across the country, one of which was Holyrood (meaning Holy Cross), then near Edinburgh. It later became the Chapel Royal, and burial place of many Scottish monarchs. Though it is now roofless, people come to see its ruined arches and marvel at the faith which inspired such building projects and beauty.

Edinburgh would have been on the pilgrim routes to Durham (St Cuthbert), Dunfermline (St Margaret) and, greatest of all, St Andrews, but other pilgrims came to the Edinburgh area itself to visit Restalrig and St Triduana's well, which is still there for us to visit (54). The hexagonal medieval chapel originally pulsated with water from the hidden springs, and bathing the eyes in it brought healing to those who flocked there.

The Reformation witnessed many changes and new ideas about religion, but people still hankered after 'holy places'. In the Greyfriars Church (6) people gathered to sign the National Covenant in 1638, and ever since it has been visited in its honour; nearby in the churchyard is the 'Covenanters' Prison', where committed believers were imprisoned for the beliefs that they held so firmly. The graveyard itself and the wording of the inscriptions of the great, good and ordinary citizens of the past link us with the Scots of old. We wonder if our own forebears are perhaps buried here. To find a stone with one's own family name on it, in a graveyard, such as surround so many churches, is, of course, particularly satisfying.

In medieval times St Giles Church (1), the spiritual heart of Edinburgh, was filled with altars in honour of the saints, both Scottish and beyond; St Ninian, St Columba, St John, St Nicholas, and many more. It became a Cathedral under King Charles I, and was the setting both for his coronation and the revolt at his new Prayer Book services. St Giles is still the setting for many great ceremonies of state and church. Its Scottish crown steeple rising above the city marks its significance and draws people to visit, and to think of the faith that has inspired the nation for so many centuries, and still does so today.

Nearby, hidden in Carrubber's Close, is Old St Paul's Church (8), the home of a congregation of Scottish Episcopalians, whose origins lie in the congregation of St Giles who were turned out in 1688 when bishops were abolished from the Church of Scotland. Here, Prince Charles Edward is said to have been proclaimed Regent in 1745, and later, in days of persecution for Jacobitism, a medical student was led secretly in the dark, for worship. He became the first Bishop in the United States of America, and there is a chapel in his honour in the church.

In the New Town of Edinburgh are several magnificent churches dating from the days of the Scottish Enlightenment, none finer than St Andrew's and St George's (15) in George Street. It was the setting in 1843 for the great Disruption in the Church of Scotland, when, on a point of religious principle, a huge number of ministers and people left the security of the Established

Church to form the Free Church of Scotland. Although, after the differences were largely healed, there was a great reunion, many remained in the Free Church which still has its headquarters in Edinburgh, and to visit St Columba's Free Church is to feel that the days of covenanted Presbyterianism are still here.

Modern-day pilgrims may find themselves drawn to the vast and cavernous but welcoming St Mary's Episcopal Cathedral, Palmerston Place (**18**), whose three spires are the dominant feature of the West End of Edinburgh. Here, as was normal in the distant past but now uniquely in Scotland, one can listen to the daily services, sung chorally by a full choir, drawn from the nearby St Mary's Music School.

In the tradition of old, pilgrims of today who visit St Mary's Metropolitan Cathedral (**11**) can venerate a relic of St Andrew, the patron saint of Scotland, gifted by the Pope in 1879. When visiting St Patrick's Church (**9**) in the Old Town, one can see the shrine of Margaret Sinclair (Sister Mary Francis of the Five Wounds), 1900–25, the 'Edinburgh Wonder Worker', who was declared 'Venerable' by the Vatican in 1978.

Finally, in visiting Rosslyn Chapel (**91**), one is following crowds of modern-day pilgrims who make their way to this unique structure, which has miraculously survived unscathed for more than 500 years. The legends attached to the building and the possibility of hidden meanings fascinate people, but it is the intention of the congregation who worship there that all visitors should not only marvel at it, but be aware of the faith that lay behind its building and still inspires people today.

May God bless everyone who turns aside from the pressures of life to visit some of the sacred places detailed in this book, finding refreshment of spirit and inspiration in each and every one of them.

CANON ALLAN MACLEAN
St Mary's Episcopal Cathedral, Edinburgh

Introduction

Edinburgh and Midlothian

Edinburgh is Scotland's capital city and has been for centuries. Its strategic importance was for much of that time based on its castle rock, and its site on a narrow strip of low land between the Pentland Hills and the Firth of Forth. Midlothian (originally known as Edinburghshire) is its effective hinterland, source historically of much of its food, and most of the fuel (coal) that sustained it. The town was for centuries on a very restricted site, extending east from the castle rock to the boundary with the separate burgh of Canongate, and bounded on the north and south by deep valleys. This resulted in a high density of building, and also in extremes of wealth and poverty. Once confirmed as *the* capital it became (with the Canongate) the principal residence of the court, and hence the administrative and legal centre for Scotland, attracting the leading landowners to live here for at least part of the year, and providing a base for merchants, tradesmen and artists of all kinds serving the court and the nobles. Its parish church was St Giles.

The town absorbed the Canongate in 1856, but had begun to develop to the south by the middle of the eighteenth century. In the 1750s, the Town Council took the bold step of planning a very large 'New Town' on a ridge to the north of the castle rock. This took several decades to complete, and provided a focus for several satellite developments. All of these required – and received – new church buildings. All were focused on housing the expanding middle and upper classes.

Fig. 1. The former Carrington Parish Church, Midlothian

As what had become a city expanded further throughout the nineteenth century, this pattern of separating the middle and upper classes from the working classes continued, with the areas allocated to working-class housing densely built up. This resulted in the building of churches designed to serve parishes of very different character. By 1900, Edinburgh had become significantly industrialised, with lead status in brewing and printing, and in biscuit-baking, but industry was not an integral part of the community – a source of civic pride – as it was in

Fig. 2. Newton Parish Church, Edinburgh

Glasgow, or Dundee, or any one of a number of other large Scottish towns. This phenomenon had important repercussions for church building, and one cannot, therefore, ignore it. Nor too, should one forget Midlothian's status as a dependency of the capital, with the county town being the city.

Because Edinburgh did not rely solely on industry for its economic base it survived the depressions of the interwar

Fig. 3. St Mungo's Parish Church, Penicuik, Midlothian

years relatively unscathed, and continued to expand by the construction of local authority housing schemes and bungalow suburbs. The process of urban expansion resumed after 1945, as elsewhere in Scotland, with the construction of new working-class housing schemes on the periphery of the city. In Midlothian, expansion of deep mining for coal necessitated the building of new mining villages.

The area has a very varied collection of church buildings, some of exceptional historical interest. There is a tradition that a mission was established by the seventh-century St Cuthbert on or near the site of the present St Cuthbert's Church (22). From the medieval period there are

Fig. 4. The former Catholic Apostolic Church, Broughton Street, Edinburgh

Fig. 5. The former Newington and St Leonard's Parish Church, Edinburgh

still four churches with substantial twelfth-century remains still in use, at Edinburgh Castle, Dalmeny, Duddingston and Kirkliston. The tiny chapel of St Margaret in Edinburgh Castle (**2**) is a gem. The others are all parish churches. Of these Dalmeny (**71**) is the least altered, and is the most complete early Romanesque church in Scotland. Duddingston (**50**) is substantially of the twelfth century, and Kirkliston (**73**) has an exceptionally fine doorway of the period. The abbey of Holyrood was founded in the twelfth century, but the surviving part, the roofless nave, is later, and has been much altered. Of the later medieval period, the Kirk of St Giles (**1**) is the largest and most elaborate, but it has been substantially altered, and apart from its superb crown steeple, much of its interest now lies in later work. Other fifteenth-century buildings in Edinburgh are the relocated and altered Trinity College Church, off the Royal Mile, and the remains of the chapel of St Triduana at Restalrig (next to St Margaret's Church, **54**). The fifteenth-century Carmelite Friary Church (now a Scottish Episcopal Church) at South Queensferry (**77**) is a unique survival of its type in Scotland. Corstorphine Old Parish Church (**67**) is also largely of fifteenth-century date, and, like the South Queensferry building roofed with stone slabs. In Midlothian, there are three fine fifteenth-century churches, all of which were adapted for Reformed worship after the Reformation. The most complete is Crichton Collegiate Church (**83**), of which the nave was apparently never completed. The church at Temple is now roofless, but a pleasing, simple building. St Nicholas Buccleuch Church in Dalkeith (**86**) had its nave

Fig. 6. The Sacred Heart Roman Catholic Church, Edinburgh

and transepts substantially restored in 1854, but the choir was left unroofed and decaying. A trust has recently been formed to consolidate the choir.

The outstanding seventeenth-century churches in the area are Greyfriars Tolbooth and Highland (**6**, 1620 on), Tron (1637–47 on) and Canongate (**10**, c.1690), in Edinburgh, along with the old parish churches of Cramond (**59**, 1656), South Queensferry (1633) and Glencorse (1665), though only Cramond is still a church in use as such. Greyfriars has had a very complex building history, and the Tron church has been much altered, but Canongate is largely in its original condition. It is the first church in Scotland, apart from the Chapel Royal in Stirling, to exhibit classical features.

Fig. 7. The former St Stephen's Parish Church, Edinburgh

There are few surviving early eighteenth-century churches in the area. Carrington (1710, Fig. 1) is no longer a church, but Newbattle (**87**, 1727) is, as is Newton (Fig. 2). All are simple, vernacular buildings though Carrington and Newbattle have towers with slated spires, unusual in Scotland at that date. From the 1770s the pace of church construction grew, especially in the towns and larger villages. In 1771 Penicuik St Mungo's (Fig. 3) was constructed in full classical style, at the expense of Sir John Clerk, the local landowner. It is said that he wished to include a steeple, but that this was rejected by the congregation. In 1774 a large Scottish Episcopal chapel, with a full-width portico, and steeple, was built in the Cowgate, Edinburgh. It is now St Patrick's Roman Catholic Church, but has been refronted (**9**). Several of the churches built to serve Edinburgh's New Town followed this classical model. St Andrew's and St George's, George Street (**15**), and the first St Cuthbert's (**22**), were both built in the 1780s, with classical steeples. St George's (1814, now West Register House) has a dome instead of a steeple,

Fig. 8. The Chapel, Gillis Centre, Edinburgh

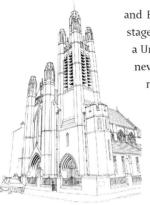

Fig. 9. St John's Roman Catholic Church, Portobello

and Broughton St Mary's (**13**, 1824) a domed top stage to its steeple. Broughton Place, originally a United Secession church, was built in 1820, but never received its intended spire. It is now auction rooms. The last classical church to be built in the New Town was the first Catholic Apostolic church, in Broughton Street (c.1844–5, now offices, Fig. 4). Outside the New Town, North Leith (**55**, 1816) and St Andrew's Place, Leith (1827, no longer a church) also had porticos. This is the most remarkable body of fully-developed classical churches in Scotland. Other classically influenced churches in Edinburgh include Portobello Old (**52**, 1809), Newington and St Leonard's (1823, now the Queen's Hall, Fig. 5), St Bernard's (1823, now Stockbridge, **17**) and Leith Junction Road (1825, originally United Secession). St Mark's Episcopal Church, Portobello (**53**, 1824), is unusual in having half-round classical columns applied to a curved central bay. Because of the resemblance of classical churches to contemporary secular buildings, many of them, as indicated above, have been converted to other uses with little alteration to their external appearance, and I have included them here for completeness.

There are also a number of other churches in the area which are classically inspired, but in which the architectural treatment is based on earlier reinterpretations of the classical. These include Nicolson Square Methodist Church (**28**, 1815), Albany Street Baptist Church (1816, now offices), Lothian Road (1831, originally United Secession, now the Filmhouse), South College Street United Presbyterian (1856, now part of Edinburgh University), the Sacred Heart Roman Catholic Church, Lauriston Street (1860, Fig. 6) and, most spectacularly and monumentally, St Stephen's (1828, now halls, Fig. 7).

The classical churches were very much in keeping with

Fig. 10. The former St Thomas's Scottish Episcopal Church, Edinburgh

Fig. 11. The former Hope Park Congregational Church, Edinburgh

Edinburgh's view of itself as the 'Athens of the North', and as a centre for rational, 'enlightened' thinking. Long before the fashion for the classical had ended, however, early Gothic revival buildings had begun to be built. These reflected, at their most thoughtful, a hankering after the pre-Reformation Church. The first of these appears to have been Liberton (**37**, 1815), at that time the centre of a rural parish to the south of Edinburgh. Liberton was a large and relatively elaborate example of the newly fashionable 'Heritors' Gothic' a style which spread all over Scotland during the next twenty or so years. St John's Episcopal Church, Princes Street (**21**, 1818) is a larger and much more elaborate exercise on the same theme, as is Cockpen (1820). Later examples include Holy Trinity Episcopal Church, Dean Bridge (1837-8, now an evangelical church), and Greenside Church (**12**, 1839, tower 1852). These churches all have towers with pinnacles at the corners, and were designed to be seen 'in the round'. Another variant of early Gothic Revival was the so-called 'English College Chapel' style, where all the architectural interest was concentrated on the front. This was particularly suited to churches in town streets. The earliest example in the area is St Mary's Metropolitan Roman Catholic Cathedral (**11**, front 1814). This was followed by Nicolson Street (1820, originally United Secession, now a community centre), and St Francis Roman Catholic Church in Lothian Street (1834, now a social centre). Free-standing churches with similar emphasis on a gabled frontage include Roslin (1826), Temple (1832, now a house), St Margaret's Convent (1835, now the Gillis Centre, Fig. 8) and St Mary's Episcopal Church, Dalkeith (**84**, 1843). The grandest early Gothic Revival church in the area is probably St Paul's and St George's Episcopal (**14**, 1818), which has 'College Chapel' gables, but also a splendid buttressed side elevation to York Place.

Of these early Gothic Revival churches, only St John's appears to be based on a thorough

Fig. 12. St Columba's Parish Church, Blackhall, Edinburgh

Fig. 13. The former Catholic Apostolic Church, Mansfield Place, Edinburgh

understanding of 'real' Gothic. From the late 1830s the Gothic Revival initially went in two directions: one was the design of churches based on a study of real Gothic, in Scotland, England, or western Europe, and the other was to use features of the Gothic in a free and innovative manner. There are examples of both in the area. As we move into the second half of the nineteenth century, urban expansion and denominational competition led to the construction of more and more churches, and though a large number of these have gone, enough survive to make a selective approach essential in discussing them. The largest and most elaborate of the churches built between 1850 and 1900 were, generally speaking, constructed by the Free and United Presbyterian (UP) churches, though other denominations also built churches of this type. The building of Gothic Revival churches with steeples was slower to develop in the Edinburgh area than elsewhere in Lowland Scotland. The oldest now extant seems to be the restored part of St Nicholas, Dalkeith (**86**, 1854), and the oldest new design Buccleuch and Greyfriars Free (**29**, 1857), by a Liverpool architectural practice. St Peter's Scottish Episcopal Church, Lutton Place (**31**) was started in the same year, but not completed until 1865. It can claim to be the first mainstream 'scholarly Gothic Revival' church in the city. Other large churches of this type are Liberton Northfield (**38**, 1869, ex Free), London Road (1874, ex UP), St Philip's, Joppa (**51**, 1875-7, ex Free), Leith St Andrew's (**1880-1**, ex Free) and Mayfield Salisbury (**39**, ex Free, 1897). The last to be completed is Dean Parish (**72**, 1902-3). The largest church in this style is unquestionably St Mary's Scottish Episcopal Cathedral (**18**, 1874-1917), with no fewer than three steeples.

The number of 'free Gothic' churches is much smaller. The most strikingly original, at least in the mid-Victorian period, are those designed by

Fig. 14. Richmond Craigmillar Parish Church, Edinburgh

Fig. 15. Fairmilehead Parish Church, Edinburgh

Frederick T. Pilkington. There are three in the area, the greatest of which is the Barclay Church (**24**, 1862–4, ex Free), Pilkington's masterpiece. Penicuik South (**88**, 1863) is much more modest in scale, but equally original, while Viewforth St David and St Oswald (**81**), which has lost its spire, is more conventional. Pilrig St Paul's (**62**, 1861–3, ex Free) is also an unusual, but less accomplished variant on the typical Gothic. The last major reinterpretation of the Gothic in the Edinburgh area is St John the Evangelist's Roman Catholic Church, Portobello (1903–6, Fig. 9), whose distinctive spire defines the Portobello skyline.

Though the classical and Gothic styles dominated church building in the Edinburgh area from 1843 to 1914, there are fine and interesting churches in other styles. These include the baroque St George's West (**20**, 1866–9, ex Free), with its Italianate campanile of 1879–81, and the wholly Italianate Palmerston Place (**19**, 1873–5, ex UP). Probably the most eclectic design is that of Augustine United Reformed Church, George IV Bridge (**5**, 1857–61, ex Congregational) a mixture of 'Romanesque, Renaissance and late Classical motifs' (*Buildings of Scotland: Edinburgh*, p. 148). The most significant variant was, however, what can be broadly defined as Romanesque architecture. The numbers of churches in Romanesque Revival style in the area was small, but they are distinctive. The oldest are probably the former St Thomas's Church, Leith (1840, now a Sikh temple) and the former St Thomas's Episcopal Church in Rutland Place (1842–3, now disused, Fig. 10) which incorporates a number of genuine English Romanesque features. Then there are the Lombardic Romanesque churches, only one still in use as such, Priestfield (**32**, 1879, ex UP). There are others in Chambers Street and in Hope Park Terrace (1875–6, ex Congregational, Fig. 11). More conventional is the Eric Liddell Centre, Morningside (**41**, 1879–81, ex UP), which uses Romanesque motifs in what is otherwise

Fig. 16. The Wilson Memorial United Free Church, Portobello

Fig. 17. St Salvador's Scottish Episcopal Church, Saughton, Edinburgh

a conventional Gothic revival design. In the first decade of the twentieth century, Peter MacGregor Chalmers adopted a more scholarly approach to Romanesque design in two churches for the Church of Scotland, St Columba's, Blackhall (1903, Fig. 12) and St Luke's, Fettes Avenue (1907–8, now an evangelical church). His St Anne's, Corstorphine (68), also for the Church of Scotland (1912) is also Romanesque, but in a variant of the style described by the *Buildings of Scotland* as 'Early Christian'.

In the later nineteenth century, both the Church of Scotland and the Scottish Episcopal Church were influenced by a desire to recapture something of the ritual and liturgy of the pre-Reformation church. Both architects and clients wanted to bring their vision of beauty of worship, and of the built context of worship, to people who they felt had been deprived of it. Early examples of churches conceived for that approach to worship included for the Church of Scotland, St Michael's, Slateford Road (**80**, 1883), and Glencorse (1883), and for the Scottish Episcopal Church St Michael and All Saints (**25**, 1867–76), Old St Paul's, Market Street (**8**, 1884), and St Cuthbert's, Colinton (1888–9). Extreme examples included the vast St Mary's Scottish Episcopal Cathedral (**18**, 1879–1917), the extraordinary second Catholic Apostolic Church in Mansfield Place (1873–85, Fig. 13) the richness and exotic character of whose design matched the heterodox beliefs of its congregation), and St Cuthbert's Church of Scotland, Lothian Road (**22**, 1892–5), scarcely less exotic, but for a more mainstream congregation. The choice of style was important – mainstream Gothic Revival for some, Romanesque for others, Byzantine, too. The scale and rich furnishings and decoration of the grandest of these buildings are clear evidence

Fig. 18. Colinton Mains Parish Church, Edinburgh

Fig. 19. Drylaw Parish Church, Edinburgh

of the wealth of the upper middle classes of the Edinburgh society of the period. Not all of these churches were on a large scale. The MacGregor Chalmers churches mentioned above were also imbued with similar thinking, as is Murrayfield Parish Church (1905). Within the same framework of thinking was the last major addition to St Giles Church (1), the ceremonial Thistle Chapel, completed in 1909, and a shrine as much to the Edinburgh craft tradition as for the Knights of the Thistle for whose accommodation it was designed.

The impact of the First World War on the Scottish economy was such that church building in the Edinburgh area did not resume on any scale until the late 1920s. By that time one could no longer assume any common approach to architectural aspiration, and the churches of the period were notably eclectic in style. St Matthew's Roman Catholic Church, Rosewell (1926) was one of a number of churches of the 1920s which introduced brick construction to church building, and this became characteristic of the later 1920s and the 1930s. Greenbank (**36**, 1927) was one of the last buildings completed by the United Free Church before its union with the Church of Scotland in 1929. It is fairly conventionally Gothic in design. Probably the most remarkable church of the interwar period is the Reid Memorial Church, Blackford (**34**, 1929-33) for the Church of Scotland, the last major 'Arts and Crafts' church to be built in the city. Other fine stone-built churches of the period, on a more modest scale, are Richmond Craigmillar (1934, Fig. 14), Granton (1934), Stenhouse Saughton (1935) and Fairmilehead (1937, Fig. 15). These were all built by the reunited Church of Scotland to serve new housing areas. The Granton church was one of a series of five churches of different denominations strung along Boswall Parkway, built to serve a model area of local authority housing. The most original churches of the 1930s are unquestionably the Wilson Memorial United Free Church, Portobello (1933, Fig. 16) built in 'Moderne' style for

Fig. 20. Craigsbank Parish Church, Edinburgh

Fig. 21 St Mary Magdalene's Roman Catholic Church, Bangholm, Edinburgh

a congregation who stayed out of the union of 1929, and the extraordinarily powerful and stark St Salvador's Scottish Episcopal Church, Saughton (1939–42, Fig. 17), Gothic-inspired, but stripped to the bone. The only other church in the area completed during the Second World War appears to have been Newtongrange (1942), built for mining families in the Lothian coalfield.

As alluded to above, Edinburgh, in common with other Scottish cities and large towns, embarked on major programmes of council and private house construction after the Second World War. New housing was also built to serve mining families in Midlothian. There was a determined initiative by the Church of Scotland and the Roman Catholic Church to build churches for these new developments, and about thirty new churches were built for that purpose between 1950 and the early 1970s. Building materials, and money, were in short supply for most of that period, but in spite of that some very fine churches were built. Most were of innovative designs, but two were notable in being inspired by seventeenth- and eighteenth-century Scots kirks. These are Colinton Mains (1954, Fig. 18) and Drylaw (1956, Fig. 19). To these might be added the Robin Chapel, Craigmillar (**48**, 1950), designed as part of a sheltered housing complex which was built as a memorial to a young man killed in 1945. Of the modernist designs, I will single out some that seem to me to be of exceptional merit. St Margaret's Roman Catholic Church, Davidson's Mains (1950) was a pioneering A-frame building, and still looks modern. Longstone (1954) and St Teresa of Lisieux, Craigmillar (**47**, 1963) are good examples of the polygonal churches of the period. Three very different churches of the 1960s and 1970s I find very powerful. Craigsbank,

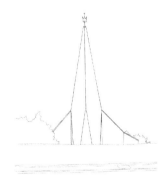

Fig. 22 St Luke's and St Anne's Roman Catholic Church, Newbattle, Midlothian

Fig. 23 St Andrew's Parish Church, Clermiston Edinburgh

Corstorphine (1964–7, Fig. 20) is strikingly sculptural, and has a remarkable tiered worship space. The exterior of St Mary Magdalene's Roman Catholic Church, Bangholm (1966, Fig. 21) is dominated by a series of vertical planes arranged with apparent, but deceptive simplicity. St Luke and St Anne's Roman Catholic Church, Mayfield (1971, Fig. 22) has a faceted white-harled spire of real sculptural quality. Other churches of notable quality of this period are St John's, Oxgangs (1956), St Mark's Roman Catholic, Oxgangs (**45**, 1959), and St Andrew's, Clermiston (1957–9, Fig. 23).

Because the Edinburgh area is so rich in church buildings, both in religious use, and converted to other uses, the foregoing narrative has had to be highly selective. Any omission is in no way intended to be dismissive. The worth of a place of worship can only in small part be measured by its obvious architectural and historic interest. Its main value lies in its sacredness, in its place as a house of God, where the people of God can encounter Him and each other. And this, I believe, matters, and matters most profoundly, not just to those who attend worship, or to believers. Places of worship are reminders to the whole world of enduring values – of the good, the true, the just, the pure, the lovely, the things of good repute – the things we all, regardless of belief systems, need to keep in our minds.

Professor John R. Hume
Universities of Glasgow and St Andrews

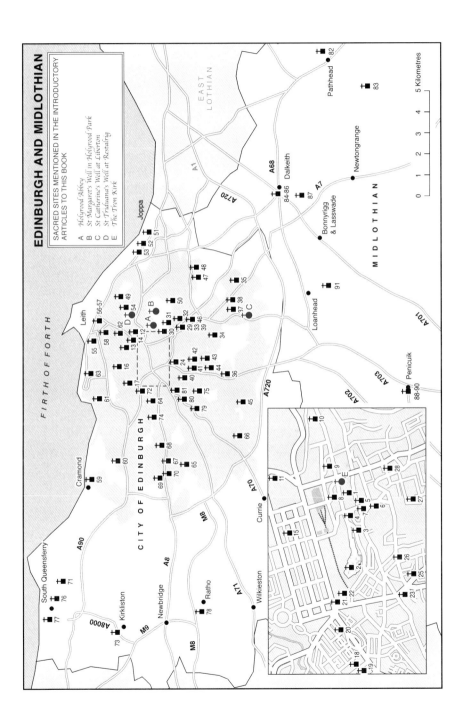

EDINBURGH AND MIDLOTHIAN

SACRED SITES MENTIONED IN THE INTRODUCTORY
ARTICLES TO THIS BOOK

A *Holyrood Abbey*
B *St Margaret's Well in Holyrood Park*
C *St Catherine's Well at Liberton*
D *St Triduana's Well at Restalrig*
E *The Tron Kirk*

FIRTH OF FORTH

EAST LOTHIAN

MIDLOTHIAN

CITY OF EDINBURGH

South Queensferry
Cramond
Kirkliston
Newbridge
Ratho
Wilkieston
Currie
Leith
Joppa
Dalkeith
Bonnyrigg & Lasswade
Newtongrange
Loanhead
Penicuik
Pathhead

A90
A8
A71
M8
M9
A8000
A70
A720
A1
A68
A7
A702
A703
A701

0 1 2 3 4 5 Kilometres

How to use this Guide

Entries are arranged by local authority area, with large areas sub-divided for convenience. The number preceding each entry refers to the map. Each entry is followed by symbols for access and facilities:

𝔸 Ordnance Survey reference

🏠 Denomination

🌐 Church website

● Regular services

○ Church events

◔ Opening arrangements

♿ Wheelchair access for partially abled

wc Toilets available for visitors

wc Toilets adapted for the disabled available for visitors

👂 Hearing induction loop for the deaf

🧑 Welcomers and guides on duty

📖 Guidebooks and souvenirs available/for sale

NADFAS Church Recorders' Inventory (NADFAS)

🧒 Features for children/link with schools

☕ Refreshments

Ⓐ Category A listing

Ⓑ Category B listing

Ⓒ Category C listing

Category A: Buildings of national or international importance, either architectural or historic, or fine little-altered examples of some particular period, style or building type.

Category B: Buildings of regional or more than local importance, or major examples of some particular period, style or building type which may have been altered.

Category C: Buildings of local importance, lesser examples of any period, style, or building type, as originally constructed or moderately altered; and simple traditional buildings which group well with others in categories A and B.

The information appearing in the gazetteer of this guide is supplied by the participating churches. While this is believed to be correct at the time of going to press, Scotland's Churches Scheme cannot accept any responsibility for its accuracy.

1 **ST GILES' CATHEDRAL**

High Street
EH1 1RE

🏛 NT 257 736
⛪ Church of Scotland
🌐 www.stgilescathedral.org.uk

The Cathedral was founded in the 1100s and mostly rebuilt during the 15th and 16th centuries. It was the church of John Knox during the Reformation and played an important part in the history of that time. The church contains fine examples of late medieval architecture and a wide range of traditional and modern stained glass and memorials. The magnificent Rieger organ was installed in 1992. The Thistle Chapel, designed by Robert Lorimer for the Order of the Thistle, was added 1909–11.

- Sunday: 8.00am, 10.00am, 11.30am and 8.00pm
- Regular weekday recitals during summer months
- Open May to September: Monday to Friday 9.00am–7.00pm, Saturday 9.00am–5.00pm, Sunday 1.00–5.00pm; October to April: Monday to Saturday 9.00am–5.00pm, Sunday 1.00–5.00pm

❷ ST MARGARET'S CHAPEL

Edinburgh Castle
EH1 2NG

🗡 NT 253 735

⛪ Non-denominational

🌐 www.historic-scotland.gov.uk

The oldest surviving structure in the castle built by King David I (1124–53). Interior divided into two by a fine arch decorated with chevron ornament. Semi-circular east chancel. Copy of the Gospel Book owned by St Margaret to whom the chapel was dedicated by her son, David I. Stained glass windows depicting St Andrew, St Ninian, St Columba and St Margaret by Douglas Strachan c.1930. Magnificent views from castle ramparts. Other attractions within the castle (Historic Scotland) include *Honours of the Kingdom* exhibition with the Stone of Destiny.

- Check website for services
- Open summer: 9.30am–6.00pm; winter 9.30am–5.00pm. Charge for entry to Castle.

❸ ST COLUMBA'S BY THE CASTLE

14 Johnston Terrace
EH1 2PW

🗡 NT 254 735

⛪ Scottish Episcopal

🌐 www.stcolumbasbythecastle.org.uk

By John Henderson, 1847, a single-nave building with a battlemented tower. Triple arcading at the west wall, originally supporting a gallery, now subsumed into a suite of rooms served by a new staircase. Stone altar, font and pulpit. Gifted oak panelling on lower east wall c.1914. The blocked east window has been filled with a mural of *Christ Enthroned* by John Busby 1959. Pipe organ, James Conacher & Sons 1880, rebuilt in 1965 by N. P. Mander and relocated in 1998 by Lightoller. Church hall, originally a school, below the church. Redevelopment and refurbishment, Simpson & Brown 1998.

- Sunday: Eucharist 10.00am, and other times as announced
- Open by arrangement (0131 228 6470)

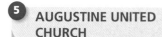

④ QUAKER MEETING HOUSE

**7 Victoria Terrace
EH1 2JL**

⚓ NT 256 736

🏛 Quaker

🌐 www.quakerscotland.gn.apc.org/

Built originally as a chapel for the United Original Secession Church (Paterson & Shiells 1865) as part of the city's Victoria Street redevelopment. Following the return of the 'Auld Seceders' to the Kirk, it became 'Kirk House', headquarters of the Edinburgh Battalion of the Boys' Brigade (conversion by Basil Spence & Partners 1960). Converted as Quaker Meeting House by Religious Society of Friends in 1987 (Architects Walmesley & Savage).

- Sunday: 11.00am; Wednesday: 12.30pm
- Edinburgh Festival Fringe events in August
- Open daily 9.00am–5.00pm

⑤ AUGUSTINE UNITED CHURCH

**41 George IV Bridge
EH1 1BB**

⚓ NT 257 734

🏛 United Reformed Church

🌐 www.augustine.org.uk

Built 1857–61 by J. J. & W. H. Hay with Romanesque, Renaissance and Classical elements. The projecting centre is carried up as the 'bride's-cake' tower, restored 2005. The Bradford computer organ of 1994 uses the pipes and case of the 1929 Ingram organ. Alterations by Stewart Tod & Partners 1995. Two stained glass windows by Robert Burns, formerly in the gallery, now the main floor. The church has an ecumenical outlook and is in covenant with Greyfriars Tolbooth and Highland Kirk and with St Columba's by the Castle. The home of Christian Aid in Scotland.

- Sunday: 11.00am
- Edinburgh Festival Fringe events in August
- Open by arrangement (0131 220 1677)

6 GREYFRIARS TOLBOOTH & HIGHLAND KIRK

**Greyfriars Place
EH1 2QQ**

NT 256 733

Church of Scotland

www.greyfriarskirk.com

South end of George IV Bridge

The first post-Reformation church built in Edinburgh 1620, altered 1722, 1858, 1938, 1990 and 2004. The National Covenant signed here in 1638. Fine 19th-century coloured glass by Ballantine, and Peter Collins organ 1990. Historic kirkyard, has fine examples of 17th-century monuments, the Martyrs' Monument, Covenanters' Prison and memorial to Greyfriars Bobby.

- Sunday: 11.00am and 12.30pm (Gaelic), first Sunday of month Holy Communion 9.30am; Thursday: all year Lunchtime Service with organ music 1.10–1.30pm
- Year-round programme of concerts and lectures: see website
- Open April to October: Monday to Friday 10.30am–4.30pm, Saturday 10.30am–2.30pm; November to March: Thursday 1.30–3.30pm. Churchyard open all year

7 MAGDALEN CHAPEL

**41 Cowgate
EH1 1JR**

NT 257 734

Inter-denominational

www.magdalenchapel.org

The chapel was built in 1541 by Michael McQuhane and his wife Janet Rhynd and contains in site medieval stained glass roundels. The panelling records gifts from members of the Incorporation of Hammermen who were patrons of the chapel until 1862. The chapel is now owned by the Scottish Reformation Society and serves as its headquarters.

- Regular services: check website
- Open Monday to Friday 9.30am–4.00pm. Other times by arrangement (0131 220 1450)

8 OLD ST PAUL'S

Jeffrey Street
EH1 1DH

NT 260 737
Scottish Episcopal
www.osp.org.uk

Off Royal Mile.

The hidden gem of the Old Town. Dating from 1884, Hay & Henderson. Entrances in Carrubber's Close and Jeffrey Street give little clue to the splendour within. This historic Episcopal church with Jacobite past has magnificent furnishings. *Still* by Alison Watt displayed in Memorial Chapel. A living church with daily worship and a prayerful atmosphere.

- Sunday: Holy Eucharist 8.00am, 10.30am and 5.00pm; Evensong 6.30pm; Daily Worship: 12.20pm, except Wednesday 9.00am
- Edinburgh Festival Fringe events in August
- Open daily 9.00am–6.00pm

9 ST PATRICK'S, COWGATE

5 South Gray's Close
EH1 1TQ

NT 262 736
Roman Catholic
www.stpatricksparish.co.uk

Between High Street and Cowgate.

Today, St Patrick's is a vibrant worshipping Catholic parish. Built 1772–4 as an Episcopalian Church, architect John Baxter. Alexander Runciman painted four panels depicting *The Prodigal Son, Christ and the Samaritan Woman, Moses and Elijah* and *The Ascension of Christ* in the apse. In 1856 the Roman Catholics took possession and a north-facing sanctuary was added, architect J Graham Fairley. Other additions were made in 1929, including a triumphal entrance arch on the south façade, architect Reginald Fairlie.

- Sunday Mass: 9.00am, 11.00am, 4.30pm; Weekdays: 8.00am and 12.30pm; Saturday Vigil: 5.00pm
- Open Monday to Friday 7.30am–4.30pm; Saturday and Sunday 8.00am–6.00pm

Priestfield Parish Church   32

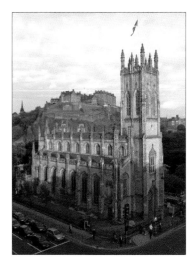

St John the Evangelist   21

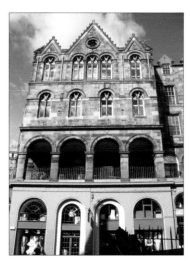

Quaker Meeting House   4

Kirk of Calder, Mid Calder

St George's West Church   20

St Mary's Episcopal Cathedral   18

South Leith Parish Church   56

St Salvador's, Saughton

Christ Church, Morningside   40

Dalmeny Parish Church   71

Interior of St Giles' Cathedral   1

Rosslyn Chapel   91

Interior of Cluny Parish Church

St Mark's, Castle Terrace

Parish Church of St Cuthbert   22

St Margaret's Parish Church, Restalrig   54

St Andrew's & St George's   15

St Philip's, Joppa   51

St Teresa of Lisieux, Craigmillar   47

St Patrick's, Cowgate   9

Stockbridge Parish Church   17

Corstorphine Old Parish Church   67

Reid Memorial Church, Blackford   34

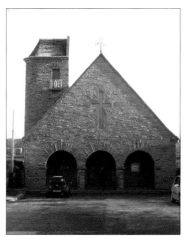

The Robin Chapel   48

10 CANONGATE KIRK

Canongate
EH8 8BN

⚐ NT 265 738
⛪ Church of Scotland
🌐 www.canongatekirk.org.uk

On the Royal Mile, opposite Huntly House Museum.

This interesting and recently restored 17th-century church was opened in 1691, its plan by James Smith being unique among 17th-century Scottish churches. Restored in 1991, Stewart Tod Partnership. The churchyard contains the remains of many famous Scots, including economist Adam Smith. 'Open Kirk' information sheets in several languages. Frobenius organ 1999.

- Sunday: Family Service 10.00am, Parish Worship 11.15am
- Open May to September: daily, 10.30am–4.30pm or by arrangement (0131 556 3515)

11 ST MARY'S METROPOLITAN CATHEDRAL

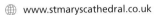

Broughton Street
EH1 3JR

⚐ NT 259 743
⛪ Roman Catholic
🌐 www.stmaryscathedral.co.uk

At top of Leith Walk.

St Mary's Cathedral occupies the site of the much smaller chapel of St Mary's, 1814. The church was created a pro-Cathedral on the restoration of the Scottish Hierarchy in 1878 and when 'Edinburgh' was added to the ancient title of the see of St Andrews, that had been vacant for 307 years. In 1886, at the request of Bishop Smith, the church was raised in status to that of Metropolitan Cathedral of the new Archdiocese of St Andrews & Edinburgh, with all the rights and privileges thereof. On the Gothic central section, at the front of St Mary's, are remains of the 1814 chapel. Organ, Matthew Copley, 2007. Cathedral Hall complex added 2005.

- Saturday: Vigil Mass 6.00pm; Sunday: 9.30am, 11.30am and 7.30pm; Weekdays: 12.45pm.
- Check website for events
- Open daily 8.00am–6.00pm

 (Café Camino 9.00am–8.00pm)

12 GREENSIDE PARISH CHURCH

**Royal Terrace
EH7 5AD**

 NT 263 745

 Church of Scotland

 www.greensidechurch.com

Off London Road.

Gothic T-plan design by Gillespie Graham 1839 with tower added in 1852, set amid Playfair's great terraces. Connections with Robert Louis Stevenson who knew it as 'the church on the hill'. Pipe organ, rebuilt here by Ingram 1933.

• Sunday: 11.00am and 6.30pm (no evening service July and August)
• Open by arrangement (0131 669 5324)

B WC 𝄢

13 BROUGHTON ST MARY'S PARISH CHURCH

**12 Bellevue Crescent
EH3 6NE**

 NT 256 748

Church of Scotland

www.broughtonstmarys.org.uk

1.6km (1 mile) north of east end of Princes Street.

A burgh church, built to serve Edinburgh's spreading New Town. Designed in 1824 by Thomas Brown as centrepiece of Bellevue Crescent. Neoclassical style with a Corinthian portico and a tall tower which is a landmark of the eastern New Town. Graceful interior with fluted Corinthian columns supporting the gallery. Unaltered organ by Lewis, 1882, recently restored. Original pulpit. Nathaniel Bryson's stained glass *Annunciation* is of particular note. Robert Stevenson, lighthouse builder and grandfather of Robert Louis Stevenson, elder 1828–43.

• Sunday: 10.30am
• Open May to September: Wednesday 10.00am–12.00 noon

A WC 𝄢 📖 👤 ☕

14 ST PAUL'S & ST GEORGE'S CHURCH

46 York Place EH1 3HU

🏛 NT 259 744

🏛 Scottish Episcopal

🌐 www.pandgchurch.org.uk

St Paul's & St George's Church has a fascinating past, but, even more importantly, a lively and relevant present. A remarkable church by Archibald Elliott, 1818, in perpendicular Gothic with octagonal corner turrets, pierced parapets and crocketted finials. Matching sanctuary added by Peddie & Kinnear, 1892. New halls and internal reordering by Lee Boyd Architects, 2008. P's and G's aims to seek, under God, to build a lively, culturally relevant and Christ-centred Church, worshipping and serving in the centre of Edinburgh.

- Sunday: 9.00 am (traditional communion), 11.00am and 7.00pm (worship service)
- Open by arrangement, contact Administration (0131 556 1335)

15 ST ANDREW'S & ST GEORGE'S

13 George Street EH2 2PA

🏛 NT 255 741

🏛 Church of Scotland

🌐 www.standrewsandstgeorges. org.uk

East end of George Street.

This beautiful elliptical church with its delicate spire and Adam-style plaster ceiling has been described as the architectural gem of the New Town. Built in 1784, designed by Major Andrew Frazer. Delicate oval interior with fine plasterwork and sweeping gallery. Two fine 20th-century stained glass windows, one by Douglas Strachan (1875–1950), the other by Alfred Webster (1884–1915). Organ by Wells-Kennedy 1984.

- Sunday: 9.00am (Communion), 9.45am, 11.00am; Weekday Prayers: 1.00pm
- Edinburgh Festival Fringe events in August. Week-long Christian Aid book sale in May
- Open all year, Monday to Friday 10.00am–3.00pm.

      (by arrangement)

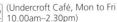 (Undercroft Café, Mon to Fri 10.00am–2.30pm)

16 ST VINCENT'S CHURCH

13 St Vincent Street EH3 5BF

A NT 249 746

⛪ Scottish Episcopal

Small Gothic gem by J. W. H. & J. M. Hay of Liverpool, 1856. It ceased parish functions in the 1960s and was bought by Lt Col. Gayre of Nigg for continued use by the congregation and the Order of St Lazarus. Since 1992 the chapel has reverted completely to parish use. Though the Order no longer has a connection with the chapel, its armorial features remain. There are fine sets of parish vestments.

- Sunday: Sung Eucharist 10.30am (Scottish Liturgy 1929), Evensong 6.00pm; Wednesday: Eucharist 7.00pm; Thursday: Eucharist 10.00am
- Open by arrangement (0131 229 1857)

17 STOCKBRIDGE PARISH CHURCH

St Bernard's 7b Saxe Coburg Street EH3 5BN

A NT 247 748

⛪ Church of Scotland

Classical church by James Milne 1823 with an Ionic pilastered and pedimented front and a small domed steeple. The interior contains the original U-plan gallery. In 1888 Hardy & Wight added the apse which was decorated in 1987 with war memorial murals by the German artist Reinhardt Behrens depicting the Lothian coastline 'at the going down of the sun and in the morning …'. Historic two-manual organ by August Gern 1883, installed here 1995.

- Sunday: 11.00am
- Open by arrangement, contact Administrator (0131 332 0122)

(18) ST MARY'S EPISCOPAL CATHEDRAL

Palmerston Place
EH12 5AW

NT 242 735

Scottish Episcopal

www.cathedral.net

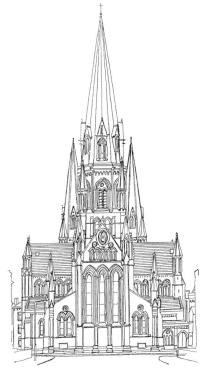

Consecrated in 1879, St Mary's designed by Sir George Gilbert Scott, is one of the world's great Neo-Gothic buildings. Its three spires dominates the West End skyline; close up, the cathedral rejoices in a wealth of ornate and symbolic detail. Stained glass by Paolozzi, Rood Cross by Robert Lorimer and J. Oldrid Scott's high altar reredos, featuring a carved Crucifixion by Mary Grant of

Kilgraston. Organ by 'Father' Willis 1879, rebuilt by Harrison & Harrison of Durham. In the grounds stand the 17th-century Old Coates House and the Song School, famous for its recently restored murals painted by Phoebe Anna Traquair 1888-92 on the theme of *Benedicite omnia opera*. The Cathedral maintains an internationally renowned choir, which sings on Sundays and for Evensong on weekdays.

- Sunday: 8.00am, 10.30 am and 3.30pm; Monday to Friday: 7.30am and 5.30pm; Saturday: 7.30am. For other services, check website.
- Edinburgh Festival Fringe events in August, concerts and other events throughout the year: check website
- Open Monday to Friday 7.30am– 6.00pm, Saturday 7.30am–5.00pm, Sunday 8.00am–5.00pm. Tours of the Song School in August or by appointment (0131 225 6293).

  (by arrangement – 0131 225 6293)

19 PALMERSTON PLACE CHURCH

10 Palmerston Place EH12 5AA

NT 241 734

Church of Scotland

www.palmerstonplacechurch.com

Opened in 1875, the inspiration for Peddie & Kinnear's design came from the 17th-century St Sulpice in Paris. A notable feature is the central ceiling motif of a dove within a sunburst. Wells Kennedy organ 1991 incorporates the oak case of the earlier 1902 organ. Meeting place for the Presbytery of Edinburgh and the Synod of the Scottish Episcopal Church.

- Sunday: 11.00am and 6.30pm (except July and August)
- Open by arrangement (0131 220 1690)

20 ST GEORGE'S WEST CHURCH

58 Shandwick Place EH2 4RT

NT 245 736

Church of Scotland

www.stgeorgeswest.com

Designed by David Bryce in Roman Baroque style with monumental stonework and opened in 1869. The Venetian inspired campanile by Sir R.Rowand Anderson was added in 1881. Two-storey galleried interior. Special features are the rose window and the pulpit. Woodwork excellent, mainly original. Organ by Thomas Lewis 1897. The first organist was Alfred Hollins, famous blind organist and composer (1897–1942). Busy church centre, Fairtrade shop and café.

- Sunday: 11.00am and 7.00pm; Prayers: Monday to Friday 1.00pm
- Open Monday to Friday 10.00am–3.30pm, Saturday 10.30am–12.30pm

EDINBURGH

WEST END and TOLLCROSS

21 ST JOHN THE EVANGELIST

Princes Street
EH2 4BJ

Ⓐ NT 247 736

🏠 Scottish Episcopal

🌐 www.stjohns-edinburgh.org.uk

St John's is one of architect William Burn's finest early 19th-century buildings (1818) with soaring columns leading the eye to the fan-vaulted ceiling. The chancel was extended in 1882 by Peddie & Kinnear who also designed the interior woodwork. Fine collection of stained glass: windows by Clayton & Bell, Heaton, Butler & Bayne's and Ballantine. Woodwork by Peddie & Kinnear, 1867. Organ originally by 'Father' Willis 1901. In addition to daily worship, the church also houses a vibrant community including One World Shop, Cornerstone Bookshop, Peace and Justice Centre and Cornerstone Café.

- Sunday: Holy Communion 8.00am, 10.30am (1st Sunday), Sung Eucharist 9.45am, and Choral Matins 11.15am (all other Sundays), Choral Evensong 6.00pm; Weekday Service: 1.00pm; Communion Service: Wednesday 11.00am
- Open Monday to Friday 8.00am–4.15pm; Saturday 9.00am–12.00 noon

22 PARISH CHURCH OF ST CUTHBERT

5 Lothian Road
EH1 2EP

Ⓐ NT 248 736

🏠 Church of Scotland

🌐 www.st-cuthberts.net

The present church, the seventh on the site, was built 1892-5, and designed by Hippolyte Blanc, retaining the 1790 spire. Tradition has it that St Cuthbert had a cell church here; if so, Christian worship has taken place here for 1300 years. Furnishings include marble communion table, murals and stained glass window by Tiffany. Fine organ originally by Hope-Jones 1899, rebuilt 1928, 1957 and 1997. Interior altered in 1990 by Stewart Tod, sympathetically reducing the seating space by one bay to create meeting rooms. Interesting graveyard, with many famous names. An oasis in the centre of the city.

- Sunday: 9.30am, 11.00am and 6.30pm (Service of Healing)
- Open end of April to mid-September: Monday to Saturday 10.00am–4.00pm

23 EDINBURGH METHODIST MISSION

**Central Hall
2 West Tollcross
EH3 9BP**

🏛 NT 248 730

🏠 Methodist

0.8km (½ mile) south of west end of Princes Street.

1901 by Dunn & Findlay of Edinburgh with the theatre-like main hall on the first floor. The main hall has a curved and ribbed ceiling on arches rising from Ionic columns. Leaded windows of clear 'cathedral' glass embellished in the style of Glasgow Art Nouveau. Lower landings are decorated with mosaic tiles. Monumental organ by H. S. Vincent, 1904, rebuilt by C. P. Scovell, 1930, and enlarged by J. W. Walker, 1958. A well-known venue for concerts, conferences and meetings.

- Sunday: 11.00am
- Venue for the National Association of Youth Orchestras during Edinburgh Festival
- Open Monday to Friday 9.00am–10.00pm

  (Dunbar Street)

24 BARCLAY CHURCH

**Bruntsfield Place
EH10 4HW**

🏛 NT 249 726

🏠 Church of Scotland

🌐 www.barclaychurch.org.uk

Tollcross, close to King's Theatre.

1864 in powerful Ruskinian Gothic, this is Frederick T. Pilkington's greatest achievement. The 70m (230ft) spire is a well-known landmark. Spectacular theatrical space within with double gallery. Painted ceiling. Organ originally by Hope-Jones, reconstructed by Lewis. Removal of centre and other pews in sanctuary with other minor alterations and the installation of spiral staircases to the first gallery 1999, by Gray, Marshall Associates of Edinburgh.

- Sunday: 11.00am and 6.30pm
- Open by arrangement with Church Office (0131 229 6810)

ST MICHAEL'S & ALL SAINTS' CHURCH

**Brougham Street
EH3 9JH**

NT 251 729

Scottish Episcopal

www.stmichaelandallsaints.org.uk

Tollcross, on road to Meadows.

A shrine of the Anglo-Catholic movement in Scotland. The church was mostly built in 1867 but the west end not completed until 1876 and the Lady Chapel added in 1897, all to designs by R. Rowand Anderson. Austere Gothic externally but the interior is a magnificently spacious setting for a sumptuous display of furnishings, including an elaborate Spanish pulpit c.1600, carved and painted altarpieces by William Burges 1867, Hamilton More-Nisbet 1901, and by C. E. Kempe 1889. Extensive collection of stained glass with windows by Wailes, Clayton & Bell, Kempe, and Sir Ninian Comper. Organ originally by Forster & Andrews, installed in 1992.

- Sunday: Low Mass 8.00am, High Mass 11.00am, Choral Evensong and Benediction 6.30pm; Tuesday: Low Mass 8.00am; Wednesday: Low Mass 12.30pm; Thursday: Low Mass 6.00pm; Friday: Low Mass 10.30am; Saturday: Low Mass 12.30pm (1st Saturday in month)
- Open all year, Wednesday 12.00 noon–2.30pm, Friday 10.00am–2.00pm, Saturdays during Edinburgh Festival or by arrangement (0131 229 6368)

SACRED HEART CHURCH

28 Lauriston Place
EH3 9DJ

NT 252 730

Roman Catholic

www.lauriston.org.uk/sacredheart

Stone-fronted building designed by Father Richard Vaughan SJ 1860, altered by Archibald Macpherson 1884. Holyrood Madonna of carved wood, probably late 16th century. Stations of the Cross on large canvasses by Peter Rauth 1874. Organ originally constructed by Hamilton of Edinburgh 1874, rebuilt 1907 by Scovell (who also designed the pulpit). A gift of fine oak panelling from St Margaret's Convent (now Gillis Centre) has enabled the Choir Loft to be greatly enhanced. Restoration and conservation 2002.

- Saturday Vigil: 6.30pm; Sunday: 7.45am, 10.45am, and 8.00pm; weekdays: 7.45am, 12.30pm and 5.45pm
- Open daily 7.30am–6.30pm

ST ANDREW'S ORTHODOX CHAPEL

Buccleuch Parish School, Hope Park Halls
2 Meadow Lane
EH8 9NR

NT 262 728

Orthodox

www.edinburgh-orthodox.org.uk

Off Buccleuch Place.

Originally Hope Park Halls of Buccleuch Parish School and built 1830s in the Jacobean style common to Edinburgh schools of the time. Edinburgh Parish was founded as a chaplaincy for Polish servicemen. Orthodox furnishings and icons. Services are largely in English; Greek, Slavonic and some Romanian are also used.

- Sunday and Feasts: 9.00am Matins, Liturgy 10.00am, Vespers 6.30pm; Monday to Saturday: Matins 7.30am, Vespers 6.30pm
- Open by arrangement (0131 667 0372 or 0131 662 1846)

 (by arrangement)

28 NICOLSON SQUARE METHODIST CHURCH

Nicolson Square
EH8 9BX

⚔ NT 261 732
🏠 Methodist
🌐 www.nicsquare.org.uk

Surgeons' Hall.

By Thomas Brown 1815, set diagonally across the corner of the square behind a forecourt. Classical two-storey front based on Adam's design for the west block of the university. Inside, fluted cast-iron columns support the U-plan gallery. Substantial modernisation 1972. Organ by Forster & Andrews of Hull dating from 1864. Interesting modern chapel in basement created in 1989 by Nira Ponniah. Small public garden at rear.

• Sunday: 6.30pm
• Edinburgh Festival Fringe events in August, concerts at other times
• Open Monday to Friday 8.30am–3.00pm

 (8.30am–3.00pm)

29 BUCCLEUCH & GREYFRIARS FREE CHURCH

West Crosscauseway
EH8 9JP

⚔ NT 261 730
🏠 Free Church of Scotland
🌐 www.buccleuchfreechurch.co.uk

Off Nicolson Street.

Built 1857 by Hay & Hay of Liverpool in Gothic style for the Free Buccleuch congregation established at the 1843 Disruption. The congregation has sought to remain true to the original Free Church vision of reformed theology and evangelical outreach. One of the largest hammerbeam roofs in the country and an impressive spire.

• Sunday: 11.00am and 6.30pm
• Open by arrangement (0131 667 4651)

EDINBURGH

SOUTHSIDE

 KIRK O'FIELD PARISH CHURCH

140 Pleasance
EH8 9RR

⟂ NT 264 732

⌂ Church of Scotland

⊕ www.kirkofield.com

Built as Charteris Memorial Church in 1912. Late Scots Gothic by James B. Dunn using the sloping site to create halls below the nave. Lorimerian vine enrichment on the vestibule ceiling. Wagon-roofed nave with west gallery. Memorial to the Rev A. H. Charteris 1908. Mission Hall 1891 dedicated to St Ninian.

- Sunday: 11.00am
- Open by arrangement (0131 228 1928)

31 **ST PETER'S, LUTTON PLACE**

16 Lutton Place
EH8 9PE

⟂ NT 265 725

⌂ Scottish Episcopal

⊕ www.stpetersedinburgh.org

Off South Clerk Street.

Early Geometric Gothic church by William Slater, its 56m (184ft) spire diapered with bands of ornament and cinquefoils. Octagonal baptistery (now the Miller Chapel). Nave arcade supported on polished granite piers. Stencilled decoration on roofs by G. H. Potts. Panels on chancel walls of Evangelists and the Agnus Dei by George Dobie 1890. Round Caen stone pulpit by Poole, stained glass by Clayton & Bell and Isobel Goudie. Organ by Frederick Holt 1856, rebuilt Scovell 1913, and Rushworth & Dreaper 1959.

- Sunday: 8.30am, 10.45am, 6.30pm; Tuesday, Wednesday, Thursday, Friday: 9.00am and 5.00pm; Thursday: 11.00am
- Open by arrangement (0131 667 1107)

32 PRIESTFIELD PARISH CHURCH

Dalkeith Road
EH16 5HW

NT 271 721

Church of Scotland

www.priestfield.org.uk

Close to Commonwealth Pool.

Built in 1879, Sutherland & Walker, in the Italian Lombardic style. Beautiful stained glass windows designed as a War Memorial by Alexander Strachan, Douglas Hamilton and Mary Wood in 1921. Other features of note are the handsome pulpit and organ gallery and a most unusual baptismal font of a kneeling angel with a clamshell, 1881, by John Rhind after original by Thorwaldsen of Denmark. Restoration of masonry and windows 2008.

- Sunday: 11.00am all year; 6.30pm September to June (2nd and 4th Sunday)
- Edinburgh Festival Fringe events in August
- Open by arrangement (0131 668 1620)

33 ST COLUMBA'S, NEWINGTON

9 Upper Gray Street
EH9 1SN

NT 265 721

Roman Catholic

A free treatment of the classic Renaissance style by R. M. Cameron 1888. West façade has a large semi-circular window and pedimented gable finished with a plain Latin cross. Oblong interior with open timber roof and semi-circular end forming a chancel and apse. The chancel arch is a later addition. Notable features include a collection of statues in the window niches. Extensive natural lighting from roof lights and west window. Two-manual pipe organ by Matthew Copley, 1997.

- Sunday: 11.00am and 6.30pm; Monday to Friday: 9.30am; Saturday: 11.00am
- Open by arrangement (0131 667 1605)

  (in halls)

34 REID MEMORIAL CHURCH, BLACKFORD

182 West Savile Terrace EH9 3HY

Ⱥ NT 261 710

⌂ Church of Scotland

⊕ www.reidmemorial.org.uk

A lofty, cruciform church with meticulous Neo-Perpendicular detail designed by L. Grahame Thomson and built 1929–33. Stained glass windows by James Ballantine, woodwork by Scott Morton, ironwork by Thomas Hadden, pipe organ Rushworth & Dreaper, and painting on reredos of *Last Supper* by William R. Lawson. Cloister court to rear with carved panel of *Christ at the well of Samaria* by Alexander Carrick.

- Sunday: 10.30am all year; and first Sunday of month 6.30pm June–September
- Regular organ recitals: see website
- Open by arrangement (0131 667 6989)

35 ST BARNABAS EPISCOPAL CHURCH, GILMERTON

4 Moredun Park View EH17 7NE

Ⱥ NT 290 693

⌂ Scottish Episcopal

⊕ www.southedinburgh.net/stbarnabas

Between A7 and A772 on south side of city.

Small modern church in housing scheme 1950. Altered in 1969. St Barnabas tapestry.

- Sunday: Eucharist 10.30am; Tuesday: Prayer Group 6.30pm
- Open Wednesday mornings

36 GREENBANK PARISH CHURCH

Braidburn Terrace EH10 6ES

⚔ NT 243 702
⛪ Church of Scotland
🌐 www.greenbankchurch.org

Junction with Comiston Road.

Founded in 1900 as the last United Presbyterian congregation in Edinburgh. Original building now used as halls. The present Gothic-style church (A. Lorne Campbell 1927) is an early example of reinforced concrete construction, with stone cladding. Furnishings to Campbell's designs by Scott Morton & Co. Current scheme of decoration by Sir William Kininmonth. Organ by A. E. Ingram 1927, rebuilt R. L. Smith 1972. Stained glass by James Ballantine, Alexander Strachan (2), William Wilson (3). Pulpit falls by Archibald Brennan, Penelope Beaton and Malcolm Lochhead. New suite of halls by Lee Boyd Partnership 2001.

- Sunday: 10.30am all year; plus 9.30am first Sunday of September-December and February-May, every Sunday June to mid-August
- Open by arrangement (0131 447 4032)

37 LIBERTON KIRK

Kirkgate, Liberton EH16 6RY

⚔ NT 275 700
⛪ Church of Scotland
🌐 www.libertonkirk.freeserve.co.uk

Sitting in a commanding position overlooking the city, a church was founded here in 1143 by David I, although there is evidence of an earlier church dating from AD 800. The present building was erected in 1815. Designed by James Gillespie Graham, it is a rectangular semi-Gothic building with corbelled parapet tower. A memorial stained glass window depicting Cornelius, by Ballantine 1905. Three striking contemporary pulpit falls and four outstanding wall hangings by D. Morrison. The kirkyard contains many stones of special interest, including a tabletop tomb to a local farmer, its ends carved in relief with agricultural scenes.

- Sunday: 9.30am and 11.00am (10.30am, July and August)
- Open Monday to Friday 9am–5pm by arrangement (0131 258 0859)

38 LIBERTON NORTHFIELD PARISH CHURCH

280 Gilmerton Road EH16 5UR

⚔ NT 280 699
 Church of Scotland

Built 1869 as a Free Church to designs by J. W. Smith. North-east tower and broach spire added by Peddie & Kinnear 1873. Interior with raked floor and an ornate arch-braced timber roof springing from short ashlar colonnettes with a variety of leafy capitals. Transepts entered by triple arches expressed on the exterior by triple gables. Virtually unaltered organ by E. F. Walcker 1903.

• Sunday: 11.00am and 6.30pm
• Open by arrangement (0131 658 1754)

B **WC**

 **39 MAYFIELD SALISBURY CHURCH**

West Mayfield EH9 1TQ

⚔ NT 266 717
 Church of Scotland
🌐 www.mayfieldsalisbury.org

Originally built as Mayfield Free Kirk 1879, this is a fine example of the French Gothic style of Hippolyte Blanc. Spire 15m (48ft) added 1894. Magnificent collection of stained glass by Ballantine & Gardiner, Charles L. Davidson, Henry Dearl of Morris & Co, Guthrie & Wells and William Meikle. Church House, orginally the manse, now houses the Mayfield Radio Unit which broadcasts to hospitals in the Edinburgh area.

• Sunday: 9.30am, 10.45am and 6.00pm September-June; 10.45am and 6.00pm July and August
• Open 9.00am–12.00noon; afternoons by arrangement (0131 667 1522)

 B   **WC**

40 CHRIST CHURCH, MORNINGSIDE

6a Morningside Road EH10 4DD

NT 245 719

Scottish Episcopal

www.christchurchmorningside.co.uk

Holy Corner, Bruntsfield.

French Gothic by Hippolyte Blanc, a member of the congregation, 1876. The apse with its gables and flying buttresses face onto the road; the main entrance is beneath the tower. Original murals in chancel and nave roof. Extensive stained glass by Ballantine and the east window by A. E. Borthwick.

- Sunday: Holy Communion 8.00am, Sung Eucharist 10.00am, Evensong 6.30pm; Monday to Friday: Morning Prayer and Eucharist 8.00am; Thursday: Holy Communion 11.00am
- Open Wednesday and Friday 11.00am–3.00pm

41 ERIC LIDDELL CENTRE, MORNINGSIDE

15 Morningside Road EH10 4DP

NT 246 719

Church of Scotland

www.eric-liddell.org

Holy Corner, Bruntsfield.

Former North Morningside Church of Scotland in Neo-Norman by David Robertson 1879–81. Dramatic intervention by Nicholas Groves-Raines 1992 and 1999 for conversion to Eric Liddell Centre which provides community services and accommodation for organisations of Christian witness. Galleries provide viewing of impressive collection of stained glass, including windows by William Wilson and John Duncan.

- Chinese Evangelical Church Services Sunday 1.00pm in English, Mandarin and Cantonese (check website)
- Open daily 10.00am–5.00pm; evenings by arrangement (0131 447 4520)

 (by arrangement)

42 ST BENNET'S CHAPEL, MORNINGSIDE

42 Greenhill Gardens EH10 4BJ

NT 248 717

Roman Catholic

The chapel attached to the home of the Archbishops of St Andrews and Edinburgh. A charming Byzantine church built by R. Weir Schultz 1907, under the will of the 3rd Marquess of Bute, to take the outstanding Italianate classical interior designed by William Frame in 1889 for the chapel at House of Falkland. Porch by Reginald Fairlie 1934. There are examples of stained glass windows by Gabriel Loire of Chartres dating from the 1970s; other windows were installed in 1999 commemorating the 1,600th anniversary of St Ninian and the 1,400th anniversary of St Columba, as well as a millennium window. The chapel contains memorabilia of the Archbishops since the restoration of the hierarchy.

- Church Service times as announced
- Open weekdays 9.00am–5.00pm

43 ST PETER'S CHURCH, MORNINGSIDE

77 Falcon Avenue EH10 4AN

NT 248 715

Roman Catholic

www.stpetersrcchurchedinburgh.org.uk

Regarded as Robert Lorimer's most innovative design, St Peter's was built in two stages: 1906–7 and the nave completed 1928–9. A tall square Italianate campanile watches over a welcoming courtyard. Sculpture on the apse of *The Crucifixion* by Joseph Hayes. The towering nave in whitewashed brick is lit by six tall windows. Stained glass by Morris and Gertrude A. Meredith Williams, Nina Millar Davidson, and Pierre Fourmaintraux. Lead font with fish motif by G. P. Bankart.

- Sunday: 9.00am, 11.00am and 5.30pm; Saturday: 12.00 noon; Weekdays: 9.00am
- Open by arrangement (0131 447 2502)

44 MORNINGSIDE PARISH CHURCH

Cluny Gardens
EH10 4DN

NT 246 707

Church of Scotland

www.morningsideparishchurch.
net

Built as St Matthew's 1890 by Hippolyte Blanc, inspired by late 13th-century Gothic. Fourteen stained glass windows on side aisles of nave, including the new St Cuthbert window to mark the 2003 union, and the St Andrew Window in North Transept. East window: *Four Apostles*, Sir Edward Burne-Jones 1900; west window: four scenes from the ministry of Jesus, Percy Bacon & Co 1905. Last 'Father' Willis organ in Scotland, installed 1901. Morningside Parish Church is a union of five churches – St Matthew's; Morningside Parish Church (Newbattle Terrace); Morningside High Church; South Morningside Church and Braid Church.

- Sunday: autumn, winter, spring 11.00am and 6.30pm; summer 9.30am and 11.00am
- Edinburgh Festival Fringe events in August, concerts at other times
- Open by arrangement (0131 447 6745)

45 ST MARK'S CHURCH, OXGANGS

29 Oxgangs Avenue
EH13 9HX

NT 237 691

Roman Catholic

www.stmarksedin.org.uk

Opened by Archbishop Gordon Gray in 1962. Designed by Peter Whiston with a slated roof above walls made of cobbles. Rich interior with timber roof and dramatic large triangular west window. Stained glass by Dom Basil Robinson, OSB. Stations of the Cross by Vincent Butler (Saltire Award 1971). Statues of Our Lady and St Mark by Norman Forrest.

- Saturday Vigil: 6.00pm; Sunday Mass: 10.00am
- Open Wednesday and Saturday 11.00am–1.00pm

EDINBURGH

EAST

 CRAIGMILLAR PARK CHURCH

Mayfield Church
2C Craigmillar Park
EH16 5LZ

 NT 269 715

Church of Scotland

www.craigmillarpark.org

Adjacent to Royal Blind School in South Newington.

Cruciform Gothic-style church in cream sandstone, 1879, by Hardy & Wight. Major alterations to the chancel in 1957 by Ian G. Lindsay, and, in 2004, dedication of a chapel created under the gallery. Organ built as two-manual in 1894 by Brindley & Foster, enlarged to three-manual in 1920s by Ingram & Co. Various stained glass windows from 1920s to 2004 including lights by Margaret Chilton and Marjorie Kemp. New stone cross erected on roof, 2008.

- Sunday: 10.30 am
- Open by arrangement (0131 667 1623)

 ST TERESA OF LISIEUX, CRAIGMILLAR

120 Niddrie Mains Road
EH16 4EG

NT 295 716

Roman Catholic

Octagonal church with pebble-dashed walls, green copper roof topped by a cross. Designed by architect Charles W. Gray, it was opened in 1963. Stone statue of St Teresa above the main entrance. Pipe organ. Redecorated 2002. In the weekday chapel is a copy of the San Damiano crucifix, a reminder that the church has been staffed since its opening by Franciscan Friars.

- Saturday Vigil: 6.00pm; Sunday: 10.30am; Monday to Friday: 9.30am; Saturday: 10.00am
- Open by arrangement (0131 661 2185)

48 THE ROBIN CHAPEL

**Thistle Foundation
Niddrie Mains Road
EH16 4AE**

🜊 NT 295 715

⛪ Ecumenical

🌐 www.robinchapel.org.uk

Memorial to Robin Tudsbery, killed in the last days of the Second World War, built by Architect John F. Matthew 1950, at the centre of a housing complex for war-wounded service personnel and their families. Peaceful and secluded interior enhanced by stone capitals carved by Maxwell Adam, wood carvings by Thomas Good and wrought-iron work by James Finnegan. Finely detailed stained glass by Sadie McLellan, depicting scenes from Bunyan's *Pilgrim's Progress*, restored 2005. This ecumenical chapel is open to all.

• Sunday: 4.30pm Evening Sung Service
• Open by arrangement (0131 661 3366)

 (by arrangement)

49 ST CHRISTOPHER'S, CRAIGENTINNY

**Craigentinny Road
EH7 6RL**

🜊 NT 292 748

⛪ Church of Scotland

Built by James McLachlan in 1934–8, the foundation stone was laid by John Buchan, author of *The Thirty Nine Steps*. The exterior is of variegated red brick with round arched windows and tiled roof. The interior is a darker plum-coloured brick with a low wagon roof and segmental arches. The organ, Ingram 1900, came from St Catherine's Argyll and was installed here in 1969. There are two stained glass windows by Sax Shaw and one by George Reid.

• Sunday: 10.30am; Communion on last Sunday in January, March, June and October; short Communion after Family Services on the first Sunday of the month
• Open Tuesdays and Saturdays 10.00am–12.00 noon, or by arrangement (0131 669 2129)

50 DUDDINGSTON KIRK

Old Church Lane
Duddingston Village
EH15 3PX

⚔ NT 284 726

⛪ Church of Scotland

🌐 www.duddingston-kirk.org.uk

Twelfth-century Duddingston Kirk is one of the oldest churches used for regular worship in Scotland. The present appearance follows alterations in the 17th and 18th centuries and a careful and respectful restoration by Robert Rowand Anderson in 1889. Sir Walter Scott was an Elder. The painter Turner was a visitor, and Minister John Thomson was himself a notable landscape painter. The founding family of the Pinkerton Detective Agency is commemorated in a stained glass window. Duddingston Loch is the birthplace of the rules of curling.

- Sunday: 10.00am and 11.30am
- Edinburgh Festival Fringe events in August, concerts at other times
- Open August Thursday and Saturday 1.00-4.00pm, or by arrangement (0131 661 4240)

 (by arrangement)

51 ST PHILIP'S, JOPPA

Abercorn Terrace, Joppa
EH15 2DH

⚔ NT 313 736

⛪ Church of Scotland

🌐 www.stphilips.co.uk

A really striking edifice in the Early Decorated style by J. Honeyman 1877. Ravaged by fire 1998 and fully restored. Broach spire 52m (170ft) over a lofty belfry. Aisled nave with entry in the south gable. Inside, a remarkably complete interior. Clustered piers with leafy capitals support the nave arcade; foliated corbels on the clerestory support the wood-lined tunnel-roof. Fine stained glass windows to aisles.

- Sunday: 11.00am
- Open by arrangement (0131 669 3641)

52 PORTOBELLO OLD PARISH CHURCH

**Bellfield Street
EH15 2BP**

 NT 309 738

Church of Scotland

Off Portobello High Street.

The oldest church in Portobello, built 1809 by William Sibbald, in classical style with a pediment. The clock tower was added in 1839. Organ by Peter Conacher 1873, rebuilt by Henry Willis 1984. Furniture of Austrian oak. Mort safe and interesting memorials in graveyard. Public swimming baths and safe, sandy beach at end of the street.

- Sunday: 11.00am; meditation (5 minutes) weekdays at noon
- Open Monday to Friday all year 10.00am–2.00pm

53 ST MARK'S, PORTOBELLO

**287 High Street
EH15 2QE**

NT 308 737

Scottish Episcopal

 www.saintmarksportobello.org

One of the first Episcopal churches to be built in the Edinburgh area, St Mark's is a villa-like neoclassical church, square in plan, of 1824, most notable for its dome and semi-circular Doric porch. The Venetian windows and chancel were added by Hay & Henderson in 1892. Stained glass by Ballantine & Sons of the *Good Samaritan* and *The soul of Jonathan knit with the soul of David*. Organ, 1828 by D. & T. Hamilton, relocated by Ingram 1899.

- Sunday: Eucharist 8.30am and 10.30am; Thursday: 10.00am
- Open first Saturday of each month (except January) 9.00am–2.00pm

ST MARGARET'S PARISH CHURCH, RESTALRIG

**St Triduana's Chapel
27 Restalrig Road South
EH7 6EA**

⚊ NT 284 745

⛪ Church of Scotland

Rebuilt by William Burn 1836 on the foundations of the previous 15th-century church. The flowing window tracery follows the original design, stained glass by William Wilson 1966. Attached to the south-west corner is the hexagonal St Triduana's Chapel, once the lower storey of a two-tier chapel built for James III about 1477. The vault springs from a central pier, its six shafts topped by foliate capitals. Notable 17th- and 18th-century monuments in the graveyard.

- Sunday: 10.30am; Wednesday, short act of worship 1.00pm
- Open Wednesday 12.00 noon–2.00pm, or by arrangement (0131 554 7400)

     (by arrangement)

55 NORTH LEITH PARISH CHURCH

**Madeira Street, Leith
EH6 4AW**

⚊ NT 263 765

⛪ Church of Scotland

🌐 www.northleith.freeserve.co.uk

Off Ferry Road, close to Leith Library.

Classical building with portico and spire by William Burn 1816. Renovated Ian G. Lindsay & Partners 1950, and Stewart Tod & Partners 1993. Impressive two-storey 'country house' front. Light interior with galleries supported by Ionic columns. Stained glass James Ballantine. Three-manual pipe organ, built by Wadsworth of Manchester 1880. Small graveyard and garden.

- Sunday: 11.00am all year; 6.30pm (excluding July and August)
- Open by arrangement (0131 553 7378)

56 SOUTH LEITH PARISH CHURCH

**Kirkgate, Leith
EH6 6BJ**

🏛 NT 271 761

⛪ Church of Scotland

🌐 www.slpc.co.uk

At the foot of Leith Walk.

A church was erected in 1483 as a chapel attached to the collegiate Church of Restalrig. The present building dates from 1847, built to a design by Thomas Hamilton. Tower and porch incorporate coats of arms of four successive Scottish monarchs. Fine hammerbeam roof. Italian marble pulpit. Stained glass and emblems of the Trade Guilds. Organ by Brindley & Foster 1887. Set in ancient graveyard with interesting monuments.

- Sunday: 11.00am all year; and 9.30am June to July
- Open Thursdays 12.30–1.30pm, or by arrangement (0131 554 2578)

57 ST MARY STAR OF THE SEA, LEITH

**106 Constitution Street Leith
EH6 6AW**

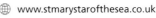

🏛 NT 272 762

⛪ Roman Catholic

🌐 www.stmarystarofthesea.co.uk

Access from Constitution Street or New Kirkgate.

E. W. Pugin and Joseph A. Hansom's church of 1854 had no chancel, no north aisle and was orientated to the west. The north aisle was added in 1900 and the chancel in 1912 when the church was turned round and the present west entrance made. Inside, the church has simple pointed arcades and a high braced collar roof. Organ originally by Brindley & Foster 1897.

- Saturday Vigil: 6.00pm; Sunday: 10.00am and 11.30am; Monday: 9.00am ecumenical service; Tuesday to Friday: 9.00am Mass; Saturday: 9.00am ecumenical service
- Open Monday to Friday 9.00–11.00am, Saturday 9.00–11.30am, Sunday 9.00am–12.30pm

EBENEZER UNITED FREE CHURCH, LEITH

**31 Bangor Road
EH6 5JX**

Å NT 266 764

 United Free Church

South from Great Junction Street.

The Ebenezer congregation was founded in 1891. The original church building in Great Junction Street was demolished in 1979 to make way for new housing. The present building, by Sir Frank Mears & Partners, was opened in 1984. Unassuming building topped with a geometric framework supporting a cross.

- Sunday: 11.00am and 6.30pm
- Open first Saturday of each month 10.00am–12.00 noon

 CRAMOND KIRK

**Cramond Glebe Road
EH4 6NS**

Å NT 190 768

Church of Scotland

⊕ www.cramondkirk.org.uk

Off Whitehouse Road, Cramond.

A cruciform kirk of 1656 with 15th-century tower. Interior altered 1701, 1811, large reconstruction 1911 by Donald McArthy and James Mather. Pitch-pine hammerbeam roof, oak furnishings, white marble font. Burgerhuys bell 1619. Jock Howieson mosaic. Plan of kirkyard available. Roman settlement remains nearby.

- Sunday: 8.45am and 10.00am, 7.00pm (1st Sunday)
- Open daily during Edinburgh Festival, 2.00–5.00pm, or by arrangement (0131 336 2036)

(during Edinburgh Festival)

60 DAVIDSON'S MAINS PARISH CHURCH

**1 Quality Street
EH4 5BB**

NT 207 752

Church of Scotland

www.dmpc.org.uk

Off Queensferry Road.

Originally Cramond Free Church. A small T-plan kirk with flat Gothic windows by David Cousin 1843. The timber bellcote with a prickly slated hat was added to the centre gable in 1866. Interior enlarged to the north in 1970. Major refurbishment to the chancel area in 1999. To the east the little school and house by Robert R. Raeburn 1846 were extended with a hall by Auldjo Jamieson & Arnott 1933 maintaining the domestic scale by means of a dormered roof. Essentially a village church.

• Sunday: 10.30am and 6.30pm
• Open Tuesday to Thursday 10.00am–1.30pm

 (Tues, Wed, Thurs 10.00am–1.30am)

61 EDINBURGH SEVENTH-DAY ADVENTIST CHURCH

**61 Boswall Parkway
Granton
EH5 2PP**

NT 235 767

Seventh Day Adventist

www.adventist-scotland.co.uk

This church was built as Granton Congregational Church. It subsequently became Granton United Reformed Church. In recent years, the building has passed to the Seventh Day Adventist Church, and now is home to their only congregation in Edinburgh. Simple Gothic building with side aisles and clerestory windows. The church is blessed with visitors from all over the world.

• Saturday: 10.00am (Bible Study) and 11.15am (Worship Service)
• Open by arrangement (01764 653257)

62 PILRIG ST PAUL'S CHURCH

**Pilrig Street
EH6 5AH**

NT 266 752

Church of Scotland

www.pilrigstpauls.org.uk

Junction with Leith Walk.

Splendid church in French Gothic style by Peddie & Kinnear, 1861–3. Gothic spire with chiming clock at the south corner. A spectacular interior with leafy stone capitals carrying a diagonal arch-braced roof of laminated timber. Windows by Ballantine & Son and Field & Allen. The chancel furnishings make an impressive pitch-pine Gothic display beneath the organ by Forster & Andrews, 1903.

- Sunday: 11.00am
- Open Tuesday and Thursday 11.00am–1.00pm; or by arrangement (0131 552 9652)

 (by arrangement)

63 WARDIE PARISH CHURCH

**29 Primrose Bank Road
EH5 3JE**

NT 246 768

Church of Scotland

www.wardie.org.uk

A jolly Gothic-style church with Francophile detail, by John McLachlan 1892. Distinctive silhouette with central lantern and conical pinnacles. Inside, a clear-span tunnel roof. A complete and perfect set of Gothic oak furnishings by Scott Morton & Co 1935 including the organ case (organ by Rushworth & Dreaper).

- Sunday: 11.00am; 10.30am, July and August
- Open Tuesday, Thursday and Friday 9.00am–12.00 noon)

64 ST ANDREW'S CHURCH, BELFORD

**77 Belford Road
EH4 3DS**

NT 235 740

Roman Catholic

**Linked with St Andrew Belford,
St John Corstorphine**

Erected in 1902, St Andrew's is a rare, virtually unaltered, example of timber church architecture in Scotland which has maintained its material quality for over a century, with lead glazing, plain tiles and bellcote externally, columns, roof structure and light fixtures internally. Central panel of stained glass in west window dated 1960 by Felix McCulloch. 17th-century German polychromed statue of *The Madonna and Child* to left of west window.

- Sunday: 9.15am
- Open by arrangement (0131 334 1693)

65 CARRICK KNOWE PARISH CHURCH

**Saughton Road North
EH12 7DR**

NT 203 721

Church of Scotland

Built in 1953, of Norman design with a strong Scottish character. The last postwar church to be built of stone – the external walls of Blaxter dressed stone, and Darney rubble, both from Northumberland quarries. Furnishings in Scottish Border oak, commissioned by the Church of Scotland as part of their exhibit for the Empire Exhibition in Glasgow of 1938 – beautiful examples of ecclesiastical craftsmanship. Baptismal bowl gifted by Her Majesty Queen Elizabeth The Queen Mother. Tapestry, Dovecot Studios, Edinburgh. Organ installed by Ronald Smith 1973.

- Sunday: 11.00am September-June; 10.30am July and August
- Open by arrangement, contact Church Office (0131 334 1505), Monday to Friday 9.15–11.15am

66 COLINTON PARISH CHURCH

St Cuthbert's
Dell Road
EH13 0JR

⚔ NT 216 692

⛪ Church of Scotland

🌐 www.colinton-parish.com

Colinton village, beside Water of Leith.

The church of 1650 was rebuilt in 1771 and enlarged by David Bryce in 1837. Sydney Mitchell transformed the building in a Neo-Byzantine style between 1907 and 1908. Mitchell adorned the semi-circular apse with murals and fine woodwork including the pulpit, communion table and rood-screen. To the south of the church, Page and Park have built new rooms which, through their contemporary design, embrace the wonderful woodland setting. The Offertory House of 1807 heralds this most interesting of buildings with its ancient graveyard set within a bend of the Water of Leith.

- Sunday: 9.30am and 11.00am
- Open Monday to Friday 9.00am–4.00pm, or by arrangement with Church Office (0131 441 2232)

67 CORSTORPHINE OLD PARISH CHURCH

Kirk Loan
EH12 7ST

⚔ NT 201 728

⛪ Church of Scotland

Interesting 15th-century church with tower, pre-Reformation relics, Scottish heraldic panels and fine medieval tombs, including those of the founders Sir Adam Forrester, Lord Provost of Edinburgh (died 1405) and Sir John Forrester, Lord Chamberlain of Scotland in the reign of James I. 1828 restoration and additions by William Burn and 1903–5 restoration by George Henderson. Fine Victorian stained glass by Ballantine and 20th-century windows by Gordon Webster and Nathaniel Bryson. Corbels carved by Birnie Rhind with heads derived from Leonardo da Vinci's *Last Supper*. Interesting gravestones in churchyard.

- Sunday: 10.30am
- Open Wednesday 10.30am–12.00 noon, except December and January

68 ST ANNE'S, CORSTORPHINE

Kaimes Road
EH12 6JR

 NT 206 728

Church of Scotland

www.stannescorstorphine.org.uk

Junction with St John's Road.

Designed by celebrated Scottish church architect Peter MacGregor Chalmers in a Romanesque style, the church was completed in 1912. A particular feature is the complex stone carving and the stained glass, much of it by William Wilson and Gordon Webster. The organ is a particularly good example of the work of Ingram & Co.

- Sunday: 11.00 am all year; and 10.00am in July and August
- Open by arrangement (0131 334 3188)

69 ST JOHN THE BAPTIST, CORSTORPHINE

37 St Ninian's Road
EH12 8AL

 NT 197 731

Roman Catholic

Linked with St Andrew Belford, St John Corstorphine

Built in 1964, a modern, spacious and light building, and home to a congregation of about 400 each week. Stained glass by Felix McCulloch is one of its notable features.

- Saturday: 6.00pm; Sunday: 10.45am
- Open by arrangement (0131 334 1693)

70 CORSTORPHINE UNITED FREE CHURCH

7 Glebe Terrace EH12 7SQ

人 NT 199 727

United Free Church

Off St John's Road.

Intimate, secluded, friendly little church, built 1930. Various ante-rooms and large hall, with new modern kitchen. Good grassed area for barbecues.

- Sunday: 10.30am
- Open by arrangement (0131 552 3666)

71 DALMENY PARISH CHURCH

St Cuthbert's Main Street EH30 9TU

人 Church of Scotland

NT 144 775

Near South Queensferry.

The most complete example of Romanesque architecture in Scotland. Dating from c.1130, with 17th-century additions and alterations and the tower rebuilt in 1937. Superb medieval south doorway, arch stones elaborately carved with animals, figures and grotesque heads. Historic graveyard. Pipe organ by Lammermuir 1984.

- Sunday: 10.00am
- Open April to September, Sunday 2.00–4.30pm; or key from Post Office (0131 331 1479)

(Sundays Apr-Oct 2.00–4.30pm)

72 DEAN PARISH CHURCH

**65–67 Dean Path
EH4 3AT**

NT 238 742

Church of Scotland

Handsome red sandstone Gothic church, 1903 by Dunn and Findlay, to replace an earlier church of 1836 on the same site. Dean Village and Dean Cemetery are nearby. 20th-century stained glass by William Aikman, William Wilson (also a cartoon), Christian Shaw, R. Douglas McLundie and in 2003–4, the centenary year, Douglas Hogg (including a glass screen reflecting the early origins of the church by the Water of Leith). Organ, 1903, by C. & F. Hamilton.

- Sunday 11.00 am
- Open by arrangement (0131 332 5736)

73 KIRKLISTON PARISH CHURCH

**The Square
EH29 9AX**

NT 125 744

Church of Scotland

www.kirkliston-parish-church.org.uk

Mainly 12th-century church of nave and tower with later additions. Two Norman archways, the largest of which was blocked up in the 19th century. Two beautiful modern stained glass windows. Organ by Ingram of Edinburgh 1925. In the 19th century a small watchtower was built in the graveyard where the earliest identifiable stone is dated 1529.

- Sunday: 11.00am
- Open by arrangement (0131 333 3298 or 0131 333 3252)

74 CHURCH OF THE GOOD SHEPHERD, MURRAYFIELD

Murrayfield Avenue EH12 6AU

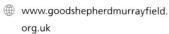

Å   NT 228 734

🏠 Scottish Episcopal

🌐 www.goodshepherdmurrayfield. org.uk

Delightful example of a Scottish country church surrounded by well-kept gardens and yet not far from the centre of a city. Designed by Sir Robert Lorimer and dedicated in 1899, the building contains some fine examples of stained glass, including windows by Margaret Chilton, Oscar Paterson and a modern window depicting *The Good Shepherd*. There is a fine Brindley & Foster organ which was rebuilt by Willis in 1967.

- Sunday: Sung Communion 10.00am; Wednesday: Holy Communion 11.00am
- Open by arrangement (0131 337 7615)

75 POLWARTH PARISH CHURCH

36–38 Polwarth Terrace EH11 1LN

Å   NT 236 719

🏠 Church of Scotland

🌐 www.polwarth.org.uk

Splendid example of late 19th- and early 20th-century architecture by Sydney Mitchell and Wilson 1901, with the tower by James Jerdan & Sons 1913. The architecture shows pre-Reformation influences, including stone carvings of the face of Mary, the mother of Christ, and several 'Green men'. Marble chancel augmented by one of the finest pulpits in the country, sculpted by William Beveridge in 1903. Ascension window at the east end of the chancel by Clayton & Bell. Pipe organ by Forster & Andrews 1903.

- Sunday: 11.00am; and others as advertised
- Open by arrangement with Church Office (0131 346 2711)

76 QUEENSFERRY PARISH CHURCH, SOUTH QUEENSFERRY

**The Loan
EH30 9NS**

NT 130 782

Church of Scotland

www.qpc.freeuk.com

Well-used and well-loved Burgh Church, built in 1894 and extended in 1993. The stone font (which now stands outside the church), the lectern, pulpit and the communion table were brought from the old parish church. Of special interest is the display of banners and the wrought-iron railings which incorporate a burning bush motif. In centre of village. Access to historic graveyard (1635–early 1900s) can be arranged.

- Sunday: 10.00am and 11.30am
- Open all year, Monday to Friday 10.00–11.30am

77 PRIORY CHURCH OF ST MARY OF MOUNT CARMEL, SOUTH QUEENSFERRY

**Hopetoun Road
EH30 9RB**

NT 129 784

Scottish Episcopal

www.priorychurch.com

Originally a Carmelite Friary founded in 1330, the church fell into disrepair during the 16th century. It was restored for the use of the Episcopal church in 1890, the work being started by John Kinross. Later work was carried out in the 1960s by Ian Lindsay. Church extensively refurbished in 2000, new floor (with underfloor heating), and a glass engraved screen to side chapel. Font cover designed by Lorimer. 14th-century aumbry. Mass dial on outside south wall.

- Sunday: 10.30am; Thursday: 10.00am
- Ferry Fair Week in August
- Open by arrangement with Church Office (0131 331 1958)

78 RATHO PARISH CHURCH

Baird Road
EH28 8RA

⚊ NT 138 710
⚊ Church of Scotland
🌐 www.rathoparishchurch.org

An interesting medieval cruciform church, with later aisles. The east aisle dated 1683, the south 1830. To the west of the south aisle is a 12th-century doorway, partially visible, with scalloped capitals and decorated hoodmould. Twentieth-century refurbishment revealed a Celtic cross stone which might suggest early worship on this site. In the south porch is a 13th-century tomb slab belonging to one of the Knights Templar who owned Ratho in the Middle Ages. In the graveyard are several interesting headstones and a panelled coffin formed of a single stone. Organ by Smethurst of Manchester 1964.

- Sunday: 11.00am
- Open by arrangement (0131 333 1732)

79 ST CUTHBERT'S CHURCH, SLATEFORD

104 Slateford Road
EH14 1PT

⚊ NT 227 715
⚊ Roman Catholic
🌐 www.stcuthbertschurch.com

Built to a design by J. B. Bennett and opened in 1896. Major renovation 1969. Significant works of art including original stained glass windows and several tapestries by the Edinburgh Tapestry Company at the Dovecot Studios, the most recent being of 1996 to mark the centenary.

- Weekdays: 9.00am, Saturday: 10.00am, Vigil Mass 6.00pm; Sunday Mass: 10.00am
- Open by arrangement (0131 443 1317)

 (in halls)

80 ST MICHAEL'S, SLATEFORD

**1 Slateford Road
EH11 1NX**

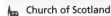 NT 234 722
 Church of Scotland
🌐 www.stmichaels-kirk.co.uk

One of architect John Honeyman's most notable buildings, completed 1883. Square 41m (135ft) tower and longest aisle in the city. Sanctuary illuminated by clerestoried nave beneath dark-timbered roof. Unusual reredos bearing Ten Commandments, Beatitudes and the Creed. Pulpit and lectern decorated with biblical fruits by Gertrude Hope. Communion table, Fall and Bible markers by Hannah Frew Paterson, dedicated in April 2001. Organ by Brindley and Foster 1895. Stained glass, including work by Douglas Strachan (1895–1925). The building has been extensively restored inside and out and provides for a variety of worship, cultural and outreach activities.

- Sunday: 11.00am September-June; 10.30am July and August
- Open by arrangement (0131 478 9675)

81 VIEWFORTH ST DAVID & ST OSWALD

**104 Gilmour Place
EH3 9PL**

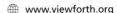 NT 244 725
Church of Scotland
🌐 www.viewforth.org

Originally a Free Church. Built by Pilkington and Bell 1871 to an orthodox four-square plan with restrained detail. The massive upward growth contrasts with the fragile shafted geometric window in the central gable. Octagonal belfry, truncated in 1976. Powerful interior, rebuilt after a fire in 1898, with very thin cast-iron columns supporting huge transverse beams over the side galleries. Organ reconstructed 1976 from two instruments by Blackett & Howden 1899 and Forster & Andrews 1904.

- Sunday: 11.00am
- Open by arrangement (0131 229 1917)

MIDLOTHIAN

82 CRANSTOUN CHURCH

Pathhead
EH37 5RF

NT 384 656
Church of Scotland
www.tynevalleyparishes.org

On A168, 0.8km (½ mile) north of Pathhead.

This charming country church stands in the grounds of Oxenfoord Castle, 12 miles south-east of Edinburgh. In the past it was destroyed twice by fire and is now a beautiful, warm and welcoming church. It was built by the architect Richard Dickson in 1824, restored in 1861 by Wardrop and enlarged in 1875 by Wardrop and Reid.

- Sunday: 10.45am
- Open Sundays in July and August, 2.00–4.00pm, or by arrangement (01875 320949 or 01875 320074)

83 CRICHTON COLLEGIATE CHURCH

Crichton
EH37 5RE

NT 381 616
Non-denominational

B6367, 3.2km (2 miles) south of Pathhead.

Collegiate church rebuilt in 1449 by William Crichton, Lord Chancellor of Scotland, infamous for his involvement in the 'Black Dinner' at which members of the Douglas family were murdered in front of the King. Restored by Hardy & White 1898 and Benjamin Tindall 1998. Fine pointed barrel vaults over choir and transepts and splendid square tower over crossing. Stained glass windows by Ballantine and Gardiner. Interior woodwork by Jones & Willis, organ by Joseph Brook & Co. Magnificent position at head of Tyne valley close to Crichton Castle (open 1 May to 30 September).

- Occasional services
- o Concerts in summer months
- Open May–September: Sunday 2.00–5.00pm, or by arrangement (01875 320341)

 (on open days)

84 ST MARY'S CHURCH, DALKEITH

EH22 2NA

🅰 NT 335 677

🏛 Scottish Episcopal

🌐 www.stmarysdalkeith.co.uk

At gates of Dalkeith Country Park.

Built as the chapel for Dalkeith Palace in 1843 by William Burn and David Bryce, chapel and transept Arthur W. Blomfield, 1890. Early English style with splendid features: double hammerbeam roof, stained glass windows by Ward & Nixon of London, heraldic floor tiles by Minton, oak choir stalls by William Butterfield and water-powered organ by David Hamilton of Edinburgh, installed 1845.

- Sunday: 9.30am
- Summer Brass Band concert
- Open July and August: Saturday and Sunday 2.00–4.00pm; or by arrangement (0131 663 4817)

85 ST DAVID'S, DALKEITH

41 Eskbank Road EH22 3BH

🅰 NT 328 669

🏛 Roman Catholic

🌐 www.stdavidsdalkeith.co.uk

Designed by J. A. Hansom and built 1853–4, the site and church paid for by the Marchioness of Lothian. Early English Gothic church with superbly decorated interior. Gorgeously stencilled coffered ceilings by C. H. Goldie. Mural of *Coronation of the Virgin* by Miss Gibsone over chancel arch. Stained glass of various dates. Organ by Hamilton.

- Saturday: 6.00pm; Sunday: 10.30am
- Open by arrangement (0131 663 4286)

MIDLOTHIAN

MIDLOTHIAN

86 ST NICHOLAS BUCCLEUCH PARISH CHURCH, DALKEITH

121 High Street
EH22 1AX

A NT 333 674

Church of Scotland

www.stnicholasbuccleuch.org.uk

Medieval church, became collegiate in 1406. Nave and transepts 1854 by David Bryce, steeple rebuilt 1888. James, 1st Earl of Morton, and his wife Princess Joanna (the profoundly deaf third daughter of James I) are buried within the choir, c.1498. Memorial monument with their effigies mark the burial site. Organ by Binns 1906.

- Sunday: Family Worship 9.30am, Parish Worship 11.00am
- Open April to October: Monday to Saturday 10.00am–4.00pm; ask at coffee shop

       (coffee shop)

87 NEWBATTLE CHURCH

Newbattle Road
EH22 3LH

A NT 331 661

Church of Scotland

Harled, T-plan church with belfry by Alexander McGill 1727. Two galleries added 1851. A remarkable number of the original fittings survive including the upper part of the 17th-century pulpit and the pilastered wooden frame of the Lothian Loft. Organ by Eustace Ingram, 1895. Good 17th-century gravestones including the amazing, ornamented Welsh family monument.

- Sunday: 10.00am
- Open by arrangement (0131 663 3896)

88 PENICUIK SOUTH CHURCH

**Peebles Road
EH26 8LX**

🗡 NT 236 595

⛪ Church of Scotland

🌐 www.psk.org.uk

Designed in 1863 by Frederick T. Pilkington in his typically eclectic interpretation of the Gothic style. Short columns support massive leafy capitals and tall pointed arches with rugged stones. The interior is crowned by an open timber roof with a complex structure. Variety of leaded and stained glass windows. Organ by C. & F. Hamilton 1901. Fully restored 1991. Short history available.

- Sundays: 11.15am and 7.00pm
- Open by arrangement (01968 674692 or 01968 674276)

89 ST JAMES'S EPISCOPAL CHURCH, PENICUIK

**Broomhill Road
EH26 9EE**

🗡 NT 232 597

⛪ Scottish Episcopal

🌐 www.stjamespenicuik.co.uk

The original church which now forms the nave was designed by H. Seymour of Seymour & Kinross 1882. The chancel, vestries, tower and bell were added by H. O. Tarbolton 1899. Excellent stained glass, including one light by Shrigley & Hunt of Lancaster and four magnificent lights by C. E. Kempe. Rood screen designed by Tarbolton and carved by T. Good; communion rails also designed by Tarbolton and carved by Scott Morton & Co. Reredos designed and executed by Mrs Meredith-Williams 1921.

- Sunday: 8.00am and 10.15am; first Sundays of the month, Choral Evensong 6.30pm
- Open by arrangement (01968 672862)

MIDLOTHIAN

90 CHURCH OF THE SACRED HEART, PENICUIK

56 John Street
EH26 8NE

⚔ NT 234 601

⛪ Roman Catholic

Originally built in 1882 as a chapel school in a plain Gothic style, it may be the only (Catholic) chapel school still in use. Considerably extended 1982 by Gilbert Gray, the curving roof connecting the old and new is quite a feature. Original Stations of the Cross by Vampoulles.

- Saturday Vigil: 6.00pm; Sunday: 10.30am; also weekday services
- Open daily: 8.30am–8.00pm

91 ROSSLYN CHAPEL

St Matthew's
Chapel Loan, Roslin
EH25 9PU

⚔ NT 275 631

⛪ Scottish Episcopal

🌐 www.rosslyn-chapel.com

Built 1450 as the church of a college established by William Sinclair, 3rd Earl of Orkney, there is nothing in Scotland to match this building. Intended to be cruciform but only the choir was completed. Famous for its lavish decorative stone carving that covers almost every part of the building, inside and out. The 'Prentice Pillar' has spectacular decoration.

- Sunday: 10.30am and 4.45pm
- Open all year: Monday to Saturday 10.00am–5.00pm, Sunday 12.00 noon–4.45pm

Index

References are to each church's entry number in the gazetteer.

Augustine United Church 5

Barclay Church 24
Broughton St Mary's Parish
  Church 13
Buccleuch & Greyfriars Free
  Church 29

Canongate Kirk 10
Carrick Knowe Parish Church 65
Christ Church, Morningside 40
Church of the Good Shepherd,
  Murrayfield 74
Church of the Sacred Heart,
  Penicuik 90
Colinton Parish Church 66
Corstorphine Old Parish Church 67
Corstorphine United Free Church
  70
Craigmillar Park Church 46
Cramond Kirk 59
Cranstoun Church 82
Crichton Collegiate Church 83

Dalmeny Parish Church 71
Davidson's Mains Parish Church 60
Dean Parish Church 72
Duddingston Kirk 50

Ebenezer United Free Church,
  Leith 58
Edinburgh Methodist Mission 23
Edinburgh Seventh-Day Adventist
  Church 61
Eric Liddell Centre, Morningside 41

Greenbank Parish Church 36
Greenside Parish Church 12

Greyfriars Tolbooth & Highland
  Kirk 6

Kirk O'Field Parish Church 30
Kirkliston Parish Church 73

Liberton Kirk 37
Liberton Northfield Parish Church
  38

Magdalen Chapel 7
Mayfield Salisbury Church 39
Morningside Parish Church 44

Newbattle Church 87
Nicolson Square Methodist
  Church 28
North Leith Parish Church 55

Old St Paul's 8

Palmerston Place Church 19
Parish Church of St Cuthbert 22
Penicuik South Church 88
Pilrig St Paul's Church 62
Polwarth Parish Church 75
Portobello Old Parish Church 52
Priestfield Parish Church 32
Priory Church of St Mary of Mount
  Carmel, South Queensferry 77

Quaker Meeting House 4
Queensferry Parish Church, South
  Queensferry 76

Ratho Parish Church 78
Reid Memorial Church, Blackford 34
Rosslyn Chapel 91

Sacred Heart Church 26
South Leith Parish Church 56
St Andrew's & St George's 15
St Andrew's Church, Belford 64
St Andrew's Orthodox Chapel 27
St Anne's, Corstrophine 68
St Barnabas Episcopal Church,
    Gilmerton 35
St Bennet's Chapel, Morningside 42
St Christopher's, Craigentinny 49
St Columba's, Newington 33
St Columba's by the Castle 3
St Cuthbert's Church, Slateford 79
St David's, Dalkeith 85
St George's West Church 20
St Giles' Cathedral 1
St James's Episcopal Church,
    Penicuik 89
St John the Baptist, Corstorphine
    69
St John the Evangelist 21
St Margaret's Chapel 2
St Margaret's Parish Church,
    Restalrig 54

St Mark's, Portobello 53
St Mark's Church, Oxgangs 45
St Mary Star of the Sea, Leith 57
St Mary's Church, Dalkeith 84
St Mary's Episcopal Cathedral 18
St Mary's Metropolitan Cathedral 11
St Michael's, Slateford 80
St Michael's & All Saints' Church 25
St Nicholas Buccleuch Parish Church,
    Dalkeith 86
St Patrick's, Cowgate 9
St Paul's & St George's Church 14
St Peter's, Lutton Place 31
St Peter's Church, Morningside 43
St Philip's, Joppa 51
St Teresa of Lisieux, Craigmillar 47
St Vincent's Church 16
Stockbridge Parish Church 17

The Robin Chapel 48

Viewforth St David & St Oswald 81

Wardie Parish Church 63